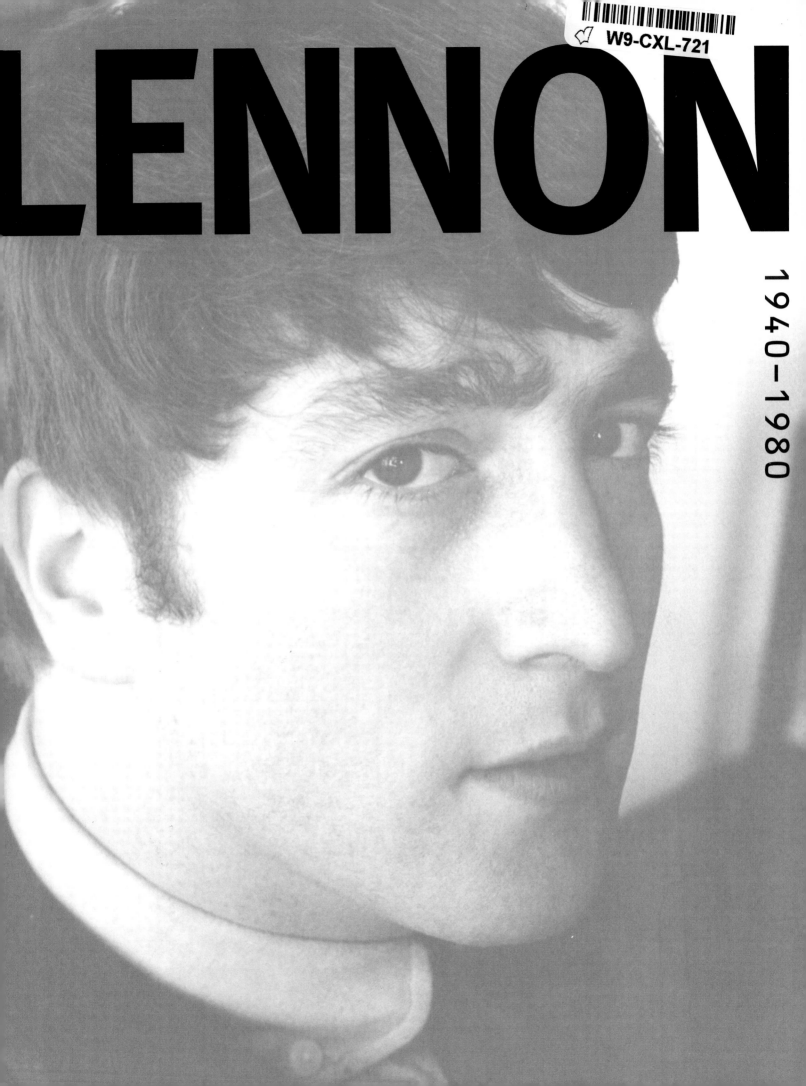

LENNON

1940–1980

2

Copyright © 1995 Omnibus Press
(A Division of Book Sales Limited)

Edited by Chris Charlesworth
Book designed by
Kalina Owczarek, 4i Limited, London
Picture research by Nikki Russell

ISBN 0.7119.4981.6
Order No. OP 47775

Exclusive Distributors
Book Sales Limited,
8/9 Frith Street,
London W1V 5TZ, UK.

Music Sales Corporation,
257 Park Avenue South,
New York NY, 10010, USA.

Music Sales Pty. Limited,
120 Rothschiold Avenue, Rosebery,
NSW 2018, Australia.

To the Music Trade only:
Music Sales Limited,
8/9 Frith Street,
London W1V 5TZ, UK.

Every effort has been made to
trace the copyright holders of
the photographs in this book but
one or two were unreachable.
We would be grateful if the
photographers concerned
would contact us.

A catalogue record for this book is
available from the British Library.

Archive Photos: back cover inset 4, back cover;
Archive Photos/Express Newpapers: back cover insets
1 and 3;
Archive Photos/Popperfoto: back cover inset 2;
Dagmar/Star File: 86br;
David Gahr: front cover
Harry Goodwin: 30
Bob Gruen/Star File: 81, 82, main, 86, 92, 93, 95, 97,
98, 99b, 100, 104, 108, 11ol&tr, 123, 124, 126;
Tom Hanley/Camera Press: 6;
London Features International: 1, 4, 13, 18/19, 20, 22,
23br, 27, 35b, 38, 40, 43, 46t, 48, 49, 53, 55, 60,
68, 69, 71tr, 72t, 77, 100br, 114, 116, 119 main, 128b;
Kieron Murphy/SIN: 2/3, 5, 82/83 insets, 84/85;
Kalina Owczarek: illustration 68;
Pictorial Parade Inc.: back cover inset 5
Chuck Pulin/Star File: 90;
Rex Features: 8, 10, 12, 14, 23main, 26, 31, 32, 33,
34, 35t, 36, 37, 39, 52, 54, 56, 59, 63, 64, 65, 66,
67, 70, 71bl, 72bl&r, 75, 76, 78, 88, 99c, 101, 102,
106, 109, 118, 119c, 121, 128t;
Star File: 46b;
Gloria Stavers/Star File: 4otr;
Virginia Turbett/SIN: 112/113;
Jurgen Vollmer/Star File: 9;
Vinnie Zuffante/Star File: 99t, 115, 117.

Printed in the United States of America by
Vicks Lithograph and Printing Corporation

introduction

It was 7.55 am, and I punched the radio awake and lay back between the covers to doze through the weather forecast. Five minutes later, the safety of the morning ritual was punctured. "This is the *Today* Programme," said the BBC's Brian Redhead with resigned urgency. "The headlines this morning: the former Beatle..." – and the time scale suddenly exploded like an accordion, to cram into a fraction of a second a turbulent flurry of sentences that ran together simultaneously through my brain. The top of the news meant death, and before the name was pronounced I knew its identity. "Let it not be John," I remember thinking, as if force of will could consign one of the other three to a premature grave.

Back in real time, Brian Redhead gravely reviewed the nightmare: "The former Beatle John Lennon has been shot dead outside his home in New York." "Only a pop singer," as my mother kindly pointed out later that day, but for me, as for millions of others around the globe, Lennon was much more than that. I'd never met him, of course, nor could I imagine a possible scenario where I might. But I knew him, or I thought I did, as far as any Beatle-besotted youngster with no hotline to the inner sanctum of the Dakota could claim acquaintance. After all, I'd bought all his records.

My shock – still the most abrupt of my entire life, other bereavements having been sadly more predictable – was scarcely unique, though in the glorious tradition of fandom The Beatles had always felt like a personal possession. But Lennon wasn't; in fact,

the testimony which emerged from 'insiders' over the next decade demonstrated that none of his fans knew the first thing about him, or his recent past. More pertinently, the witnesses even suggested that The One Honest Man Of Rock wasn't above rewriting his own history when it suited him best.

It took the best part of ten years for the aftermath of Lennon's assassination to dissipate. By 1990, when his life was being 'celebrated' by half-arsed tribute concerts and anodyne box sets, world-wide grief had been succeeded by a vague air of regret. There were still moments, usually when listening to interviews with Lennon rather than his music, when there was a mild jolt to the system as you realised that, yes, he was still dead. And the general awareness that the world was a less interesting place without him never passed away. But a decade was long

enough to realise that human life could continue without a hero – and that the hero himself had spent the best part of his adulthood racked by doubt and childlike self-abasement.

1990 was also the year I wrote *The Art And Music Of John Lennon* (also published by Omnibus Press), which was an attempt to reclaim him from the gossip-mongers and refocus attention on his work. With Lennon, more than any of his contemporaries, there was no clear-cut separation between art and life – to the point that the man's interviews were often more 'artistic' and enlivening than some of his solo records.

Researching this book, however, and listening to hour after hour of home demos and songwriting tapes, I realised that those interviews – especially the major 'confessionals' of his final weeks – were 'artistic' in another sense entirely. In short, they were

semi-fictional, a conscious effort on the part of Lennon and his wife Yoko Ono, to construct an idealised folk-myth around their relationship.

In this fairytale account, Lennon quit the cruel world of commerce in 1975, and spent five years as a perfect house-husband, baking bread, nurturing his child, and contemplating the infinite. Had he lived, the silence of the late Seventies would undoubtedly have been overshadowed by his subsequent work, and his subterfuge would have passed unnoticed.

Instead, the world was left with this creative chasm, followed by the apparently virgin birth of the 'Double Fantasy' album. The urge to fill the gap was unstoppable, and by 1990 we knew all too much about what it had taken Lennon to get through his five-year night – drugs, mostly, and terror

REVOLUTION

of the outside world.

The existence of those precious home recordings from the late Seventies allowed us a brief glimpse into Lennon's state of mind in his final years, which was then carefully disguised in time for the public re-emergence of 'Double Fantasy'. But even after the appearance of *The Art And Music*, most commentators still blithely accepted Lennon's version of events.

This book aims to set that record straight, and distinguish between manufactured myth and reality in Lennon's final interviews. But it's also a chronicle of the strangest, least predictable rock life of them all. Initially, it proves beyond any doubt that Lennon and his group, The Beatles, worked their way to the top – and remained there long after their dissolution – by undertaking a workload that makes all subsequent pop stars look like slothful malingerers. But

who would have imagined in 1963 that the cheeky composer of 'Please Please Me' would be elected Man Of The Decade a mere six years later; would be keeping company with poets, prime ministers and politicos; would be protesting against the American government on primetime TV; would be displaying his semi-erect penis to the world in the name of art; or would fall under the captivating spell of a Japanese avant garde artist for whom publicity was one-half of creativity?

Even that scarcely scratches the surface of Lennon's bizarre existence. Almost every page of this book reveals a man who was a natural born loudmouth and an insecure recluse; an intolerable bully and a sensitive proto-feminist; a peacenik and a violent revolutionary; a cynic and an unquenchable romantic.

Lennon's life was one long contradiction, and it inspires suitably contradictory responses. One moment, you start to feel that Mark Chapman's insanely twisted logic for his act of iconoclasm – that his hero was a hypocrite, and needed to be removed before he intoxicated and betrayed anyone else – had some basis in fact. The next, you're under the sway of a man whose charisma, honesty and painful self-revelation proved him to be the most compelling figure to have emerged from rock's first four decades.

What follows is a day-to-day account of that madness and mayhem. Obsessives who require the date of every Beatles show at the Cavern, or need to know which take of 'Ticket To Ride' appeared on the single, are referred to Mark Lewisohn's masterly reference books on the subject. Those who want the history of Lennon's artistic metamorphosis from teenage

rocker to avant garde experimentalist might want to read my own *The Art And Music Of John Lennon*. And if you need a Lennon biography, then try reading alternate chapters from Ray Coleman's *Lennon* and Albert Goldman's *The Lives Of John Lennon* – the first a hagiography, the second a virtual character assassination.

Meanwhile this book is a storehouse of the events that made up those Lennon Lives. Read it and weep, if you can stop yourself laughing – and spare a second to reflect on what Lennon gave us, and what he might have given us if Mark Chapman had been somewhere else on December 8, 1980. Meanwhile, as John Lennon sang from the Record Plant in New York, "Everybody here says hi. Goodbye."

John Robertson, August 1995.

John outside Aunt Mimi's house in Menlove Avenue in Liverpool.

1912-1956

14 DECEMBER 1912
Alfred Lennon is born
in Liverpool.

12 MARCH 1914
Julia Stanley is born,
also in Liverpool.

18 FEBRUARY 1933
Yoko Ono is born
in Tokyo.

3 DECEMBER 1938
Alfred Lennon and Julia Stanley
are married at Mount Pleasant
Register Office, Liverpool –
where their only son will also
be married 24 years later.

4 DECEMBER 1938
Freddy leaves Liverpool for
a three-month voyage to
the West Indies and back;
meanwhile Julia remains
at home with her parents.
The pattern repeats
itself throughout
their marriage.

10 SEPTEMBER 1939
Cynthia Powell is born
in Blackpool.

EARLY SPRING 1940
A few weeks after one
of Freddy Lennon's fleeting
visits home, Julia discovers
that she is pregnant.
She is unable to
contact her husband
to let him know.

9 OCTOBER 1940
During a heavy air-raid over
Liverpool, Julia Lennon gives
birth to her first child, John
Winston Lennon, at 6.30pm
in Oxford Street Maternity
Hospital. His name is chosen
by her sister, Mimi Smith.
On his return from hospital,
he is brought up by his mother
in Newcastle Road, Wavertree.

1941
John continues to be raised by
the extended Stanley/Smith
family, while Julia collects
regular payments which
Freddy sends from on-board ship.
Eventually, Julia suggests that
Mimi brings up the child instead.

1942-1944
John moves in with Mimi and
her husband George at their
comfortable middle-class home,
'Mendips', in Menlove Avenue,
Woolton; the couple have
no children of their own.
He continues to see his mother
regularly, though they lead quite
separate lives: she has become
involved with a serviceman
while he is home on leave from
the war. In late 1944, she
discovers that she is once again
pregnant.

C. 1945
In June, Julia gives birth to a
daughter, Victoria Elizabeth,
who is given up for adoption,
and is subsequently taken to
Sweden. Julia then resumes her
job as a waitress, where she
meets John Dykins, who
becomes her regular
partner until her death.
Late this year, John Lennon
begins to attend Dovedale
Primary School, three miles
from 'Mendips', but close to
the children's home,
Strawberry Fields.

JULY 1946
Soon afterwards, Freddy Lennon
returns home from sea, and
visits his son in Liverpool.
He tells him that he is planning
to emigrate to New Zealand,
and wants him to come along.
Meanwhile, Julia announces that
she wants John back. Forced to
choose between his parents,
John opts for his mother – only
to end up back with his Aunt
Mimi. Meanwhile, he will not
see his father for almost
20 years.

C. 1947
Like many small children,
Lennon decides to start writing
his own books and newspapers.
He inaugurates a series of
ambitious projects, which he
titles: *Sport, Speed And
Illustrated, Edited And
Illustrated By J.W. Lennon*.
John Lennon: "I was passionate
about *Alice In Wonderland*
and drew all the characters.
I did poems in the style of
'Jabberwocky'. I wrote my own
William stories, with me doing
all the things."

5 MARCH 1947
Julia gives birth to another girl,
Julia, who is John's half-sister.

29 OCTOBER 1949
Another Lennon half-sister,
Jacqui, is born to Julia, who
continues to live with John
Dykins, although the
couple are never married.

SEPTEMBER 1952
Lennon passes his '11-plus'
exam and moves on from
Dovedale Primary to Quarry
Bank High School, along with
his close friend, Pete Shotton.
He quickly makes a name for
himself as a potential trouble-
maker when he is discovered
with an obscene drawing he's
knocked off for the other boys'
amusement.
    Over the next few years,
John circulates among his
friends copies of *The Daily Howl*,
a regular Lennon 'newsletter' full
of jokes, poems and cartoons.
Some of these anarchic writings,
and their successors from his
years at college, form the basis
of his first book, *In His Own
Write*, in 1964.

JULY 1955
George Smith, Lennon's uncle,
dies suddenly. "I didn't know
how to be sad publicly," Lennon
admits later, "so I went upstairs.
Then my cousin arrived and
she came upstairs as well.
We both had hysterics. We just
laughed and laughed. I felt
very guilty afterwards."
    His mother Julia, with whom
he has maintained occasional
contact since the mid-40s,
begins to appear more regularly
in his life from this point on,
and John and Julia strike up
a relationship that is less
son/mother than brother/sister.
Among other things, she
teaches him to play banjo, and
he utilises the chords he learns
from her when he begins to
experiment with friends' guitars.

1955-1956
The almost simultaneous arrival
of rock'n'roll and skiffle on the
British music scene excites
Lennon – like thousands of
other teenagers – into believing
that he could become a singing
star himself. "Nothing really
affected me until Elvis Presley,"
he says later.

1957

MARCH
John Lennon forms his first
skiffle group, The Black Jacks,
having persuaded Aunt Mimi to
buy him a guitar which costs
all of £17. The initial line-up
consists of Lennon and his
schoolfriend Pete Shotton, but
within a few days they have
changed the group's name – to
The Quarry Men, after Quarry
Bank High School – and
expanded the line-up to include
tea-chest bassist Bill Smith.
    Over the next three months,
the ever-growing Quarry Men
leave their bedrooms and begin
to play occasionally at parties
and local skiffle competitions.

MAY/JUNE
Having begun in the 'A' stream
during his first year, and then
slipped gradually down the
academic hierarchy, Lennon
fulfils his apparent lack of
promise by taking nine 'O' Level
exams at Quarry Bank High
School, and failing them all.

9 JUNE
The Quarry Men audition for
entrepreneur Carroll Levis at
the Liverpool Empire, hoping
to qualify for an appearance on
ATV, but fail to become
famous overnight.

6 JULY
The Woolton Parish Church
Garden Fete, held at St. Peter's
Church, provides the first
documented public gig for
The Quarry Men, who play two
sets – one outdoors in the
afternoon, another that night in
the church hall. Lennon is
still the undoubted leader of
the band, which now includes
Shotton, Eric Griffiths, Colin
Hanton, Rod Davis and
Len Garry.
    Before the evening show,
Lennon's friend from Dovedale
Primary, Ivan Vaughan,
introduces him to a 15-year-old

John with George, Paul and Pete Best in Hamburg.

from Allerton, Paul McCartney. Lennon is initially unmoved, but shows signs of being impressed when McCartney reveals that he can play the guitar better than him, and also knows the words to several crucial rock'n'roll songs, for which Lennon has hitherto been improvising lyrics.

Two songs from the afternoon performance, 'Putting On The Style' and 'Baby Let's Play House', survive on an amateur reel-to-reel tape, which is eventually auctioned at Sotheby's in 1994.

MID-JULY

Lennon decides that he can incorporate McCartney into The Quarry Men without endangering his dominance of the group, and passes on the word via Pete Shotton.

7 AUGUST

Without McCartney, who is away on holiday, Lennon and The Quarry Men perform for the first time at a dingy, sweaty Liverpool cellar called the Cavern Club, which is a bastion of traditional jazz. Lennon ventures two Elvis hits, 'Blue Suede Shoes' and 'Hound Dog', and is told by the club owner: "Cut out the bloody rock!"

OCTOBER

Despite his 'O' Level failures, Lennon is accepted as a student by the Liverpool College Of Art, where he finds himself enrolled for a class in 'Lettering'.

18 OCTOBER

Lennon and McCartney share a stage for the first time, at the New Clubmoor Hall in Liverpool. Occasional dates at social clubs and local halls continue for the rest of the year, and into 1958.

McCartney reveals to Lennon that he has begun to write his own songs, and plays him a tune called 'I Lost My Little Girl'. Inspired by the realisation that rock'n'roll doesn't have to be second-hand, John starts to ape his band-mate, and soon the pair are starting to collaborate on joint songwriting efforts. "Another original by John Lennon and Paul McCartney", they write at the foot of each new set of lyrics.

Over the next four or five years, they write upwards of 100 songs, only a handful of which find their way into The Beatles' recorded repertoire. Among Lennon's earliest efforts are 'The One After 909', 'Hello Little Girl', 'I Call Your Name', 'What Goes On' and the instrumental 'Winston's Walk'.

1958

C. FEBRUARY

Another name enters the Lennon circle, as he is introduced to a tender youth called George Harrison, who happens to be a precocious rock'n'roll guitarist. Within a few weeks, he too has been incorporated into The Quarry Men's ever-changing line-up. The band continue to play sporadic gigs throughout this year, often performing for free if no paid work is available.

EARLY SUMMER

To discover how they sound, The Quarry Men – Lennon, McCartney, Harrison, John Lowe and Colin Hanton – record two songs at Percy Phillips' home studio in Liverpool. Lennon rasps his way through Buddy Holly's 'That'll Be The Day', while the group also record the McCartney/Harrison 'original', 'In Spite Of All The Danger', which is openly based around the structure of the Elvis Presley favourite, 'Trying To Get To You'.

One original copy of these recordings survives, on an acetate now owned by Paul McCartney.

15 JULY

Julia Lennon, John's mother, is knocked down and killed by an off-duty police driver on her way home from Mimi's house. "It was the worst thing that ever happened to me," Lennon says later. "I thought, that's really fucked everything. I've no responsibilities to anyone now." But he keeps his emotions hidden from his friends: "He never gave anything away," says Pete Shotton later. "His exterior never showed his feelings."

The tragedy brings Lennon closer to McCartney, whose own mother has died of breast cancer the previous year.

Mimi Smith: "He was broken-hearted for weeks. He just went to his room, into a shell."

19 JULY

Julia Lennon is buried in Allerton Cemetery.

LATE 1958

Lennon and his Art College classmate, Cynthia Powell, slow-dance at a student's lunchtime party. Lennon asks her out; she declines, and says "I'm engaged to this fellow in Hoylake." "I didn't ask you to marry me, did I?" Lennon snaps. That night, though, John and Cynthia sleep together at the Gambier Terrace flat which he has recently begun sharing with

another student, Stuart Sutcliffe. Their relationship solidifies over the next few weeks, and survives countless traumas, and secret trysts on Lennon's part, for another decade.

1959

4 FEBRUARY

The death of rock'n'roll star Buddy Holly produces in Lennon the open display of grief that he hid from the world when his mother died.

29 AUGUST

Mona Best opens a teenagers' club in the basement of her West Derby home, and The Quarry Men – Lennon, McCartney, Harrison and Ken Brown – help to inaugurate the venue. Their performance attracts the attention of the *Liverpool Echo*, which conscientiously lists the teenagers' names, starting with "John Lennon".

OCTOBER-NOVEMBER

For the second time, The Quarry Men audition for Carroll Levis, and this time they make it through the qualifying rounds of his talent search to the final at the Manchester Hippodrome on November 15. Renamed Johnny and The Moondogs, presumably in the hope that Levis won't associate them with the 1957 Quarry Men, the band turn in a commendable performance, but miss their chance of victory when they have to return home on the last train to Liverpool before the end of the show, when the final judging takes place. The group's temporary name, however, does reflect Lennon's continued, and unchallenged, leadership of the group.

1960

JANUARY
Against the misgivings of McCartney and Harrison, Lennon invites his art school pal Stuart Sutcliffe to join The Quarry Men on bass – an instrument which Stu purchases with money from the first painting he has sold to a local businessman.

MARCH
The Quarry Men tape several hours of rehearsals at a friend's house, revealing that they are far from being ready to conquer the world. Their stumbling improvisations round simple 12-bar chord changes are accompanied by early attempts at songwriting, including some mock-American rockers from Lennon like 'The One After 909'. But both creatively and vocally, The Quarry Men of March 1960 are dominated by Paul McCartney.

Around this time, Stuart Sutcliffe – whose amateurish bass-playing does little to tighten The Quarry Men's sound – suggests that they adopt the name Beatals. Lennon soon changes this to Beatles, but first the group must go through brief spells as The Silver Beetles and The Silver Beets.

MAY
The Silver Beetles recruit a drummer, Tommy Moore, but he fails to show for a vital audition in front of entrepreneur Larry Parnes and local singing star Billy Fury, who is looking for a backing group. The Beetles do their best with a stand-in, Johnny Hutchinson, but Sutcliffe's musical inadequacies doom them to disappointment. According to legend, Parnes offers them the job if they drop Stu; but Lennon remains loyal to his friend.

His commitment pays off, to a point, as The Silver Beetles are recruited to back another of Parnes' singers, the virtually unknown Johnny Gentle, on a tour of Scotland. Lennon and friends assume that fame is on the horizon.

20 MAY
The much-vaunted Scottish tour opens in Alloa. For the next nine days, The Beetles and Johnny Gentle endure lousy accommodation, sparse audiences, exhaustion, hunger and a car crash. Within two weeks of their return, drummer Tommy Moore quits the group.

EARLY JULY
The Silver Beetles are reduced to backing a stripper at an illegal Liverpool nightclub. Their career seems to be disintegrating.

EARLY AUGUST
Liverpool entrepreneur Allan Williams, who has been effectively acting as the Beetles' agent since May, secures them the chance to join other Merseyside rock'n'roll bands in Hamburg, where the red-light district is full of tough, seedy night-clubs in need of suitable entertainment.

6 AUGUST
At his mother's Casbah Club in Liverpool, young drummer Pete Best demonstrates that he knows his way around the kit. He's immediately asked if he wants to join the newly-renamed Beatles, and after a cursory audition, he accepts.

16 AUGUST
The Beatles leave Liverpool for Hamburg, where they perform their first show at the Indra Club that night. They are booked by promoter Bruno Koschmider to perform between four and six hours every night until the end of the year.

In the cauldron of a club fuelled by gratuitous violence and alcohol, The Beatles have no alternative but to shape up. Their tortuous schedule guarantees that they will survive only if they become as tough as their audience, who demand that the group play music as wild as their surroundings. Over the next four months, the tentative rockers of March 1960 transform themselves into a classic rock'n'roll band, able to jam the night away on an endless stream of American 12-bar standards. Their stamina is fired by an equally constant succession of amphetamine pills (or 'uppers').

4 OCTOBER
The Beatles' Hamburg residency switches from the Indra to the slightly more prestigious, though no less violent, Kaiserkeller. Koschmider loves them – until he receives word that they are about to quit his service for his rival, Peter Eckhorn, whereupon he hands the group their notice

15 OCTOBER
Lennon, McCartney, Harrison, Sutcliffe, and two members of Rory Storm's Hurricanes, Ringo Starr and Lou Walters, record a version of the ballad 'Summertime' in a tiny Hamburg studio.

Studio recording:
'Summertime'.

21 NOVEMBER
George Harrison is deported home to Liverpool, after someone – no names – tells Hamburg police that he is not yet 18.

29/30 NOVEMBER
Paul McCartney is arrested on a trumped-up arson charge, and The Beatles' residency falls apart. He and Pete Best are deported; Lennon stays on for another 10 days, but is eventually forced out as well, though not before The Beatles have negotiated a deal with Eckhorn for the following year.

15 DECEMBER
Nearly a week after returning to his Aunt Mimi's house, Lennon finally makes renewed contact with Harrison and McCartney, who've assumed that the group is finished.

27 DECEMBER
At Litherland Town Hall, The Beatles – with Chas Newby replacing Stu Sutcliffe, who's remained in Hamburg with his girlfriend – play a legendary live show which awakens Liverpool to the fact that they are the hottest rock band in the city.

1961

JANUARY
Pete Best's friend Neil Aspinall becomes The Beatles' roadie, as the group resume a regular pattern of gigs in Liverpool. He remains in their service to this day.

FEBRUARY
In response to a request from his college friend Bill Harry, who has announced his intention to start a magazine about the Liverpool rock'n'roll scene called *Mersey Beat*, Lennon pens an amusingly fictional account of the group's history, entitled 'Being A Short Diversion On The Dubious Origins Of Beatles'.

Lennon: "Once upon a time there were three little boys called John, George and Paul, by name christened. They decided to get together because they were the getting together type. When they were together they wondered what for after all, what for? So all of a sudden they all grew guitars and formed a noise... Many people ask what are Beatles? Why Beatles? Uh, Beatles, how did the name arrive. So we will tell you. It came in a vision – a man appeared on a flaming pie and said unto them, 'From this day on you are Beatles with an A'. Thank you, Mister Man, they said, thanking him."

21 FEBRUARY
The Beatles (rather than The Quarry Men) play their first show at the Cavern Club in Liverpool. Over the next two-and-a-half years, they perform there almost 300 times, and the Cavern soon becomes synonymous with the freshly christened Merseybeat scene – and with The Beatles.

Around this time, Stu Sutcliffe returns briefly to Liverpool, where he is welcomed back with open arms by Lennon – though not with such enthusiasm by McCartney, who has become the group's bass player in Stu's absence.

27 MARCH - 2 JULY
The Beatles' second Hamburg season, at the Top Ten Club.

12 MAY
German bandleader and producer Bert Kaempfert invites The Beatles – minus Stu Sutcliffe, who's patently not up to the task – to back London singer Tony Sheridan on some sessions for the Polydor label. They sign on the dotted line. From this point on, Sutcliffe performs only occasionally with The Beatles, and he remains in Germany when the rest of the group go home in July.

MID-MAY
A school hall is the less than prestigious venue for The Beatles' first professional recording session, at which they provide enthusiastic but hardly momentous musical support for Tony Sheridan on three numbers. John Lennon is also allowed to take the lead vocal on a rasping, innuendo-laden romp through the vintage show tune, 'Ain't She Sweet', while he and George Harrison also collaborate on an instrumental, slyly titled 'Cry For A Shadow'.

Studio recordings:
'My Bonnie', 'The Saints', 'Why', 'Ain't She Sweet', 'Cry For A Shadow', 'Nobody's Child', 'If You Love Me Baby', 'Sweet Georgia Brown'.

JULY
The first officially released record featuring The Beatles reaches the German shops. 'My Bonnie'/'The Saints' is credited to Tony Sheridan and The Beat Brothers. Despite strong sales in Hamburg, it does not, as most Beatles biographies state, register on the German national charts.

6 JULY
Bill Harry publishes the first issue of his *Mersey Beat* paper, with Lennon's witty history of The Beatles included.

Around this time, The Beatles return from Hamburg, and resume the usual round of Liverpool club gigs.

17 AUGUST
Another Lennon contribution graces the pages of *Mersey Beat* – a poem called 'I Remember Arnold', which owes a sizeable debt to the nonsense verse of Edward Lear. Over the next year or so, Lennon regularly fills the classified ads columns of *Mersey Beat* with a trail of satirical, bizarre one-liners.

SEPTEMBER
Lennon and Harrison's instrumental, 'Cry For A Shadow', is one of four tracks included on the German 'My Bonnie' EP.

14 SEPTEMBER
Mersey Beat publishes Lennon's 'Around And About', a tongue-in-cheek club-by-club guide to the delights of late-night Liverpool.

LATE SEPTEMBER
Lennon and McCartney spend £40 which John has received as an early 21st birthday present by taking a two-week holiday in Paris, where they meet up with Jurgen Vollmer, a friend from Hamburg. He persuades them to adopt the 'French' hairstyle of the moment, brushing their locks forward into a fringe rather than high on their heads like Teddy Boys.

9 NOVEMBER
Brian Epstein, the besuited manager of the Liverpool record and music store, NEMS, makes an incongruous visit to see The

Beatles at their Cavern Club lunchtime session, intrigued by the discovery that the city has its own 'underground' pop talent. Impressed as much by the charisma of the cool, swaggering, leather-clad Lennon as by their music, he begins to conceive the plan of managing the group.

6 DECEMBER
The Beatles agree to appoint Brian Epstein as their manager. In return, he promises to use his influence in the record industry, as one of Liverpool's leading retailers, to secure them a UK recording contract. Within a few weeks, he has won them an audition with one of the four 'major' labels in London, Decca.

9 DECEMBER
Just to make sure they don't get too cocky, The Beatles perform to an audience of 18 people in Aldershot, their first gig in the South of England.

1962

1 JANUARY
The Beatles celebrate New Year's Day at Decca Studios in West Hampstead, London, auditioning for the company's A&R team. Fifteen songs are laid down on tape by Lennon, McCartney, Harrison and Best, and all of them subsequently emerge on bootleg records.

Brian Epstein has emphasised the importance of presenting an attractively sophisticated face to the Decca executives, so The Beatles have prepared a repertoire which leans heavily on McCartney's penchant for ballads and standards. Sadly, Paul tries too hard with his vocals, while Lennon suffers the opposite problem, limping through Chuck Berry's 'Memphis' with a lack of confidence heard nowhere else in his recorded work. His renditions of The Teddy Bears' 'To Know Her Is To Love Her' and Barrett Strong's 'Money' are only marginally more impressive, and he sounds most at ease when performing his own 'Hello Little Girl'. It is left

to George Harrison to come up with the most impressive set of vocal performances.

Understandably, Decca's Mike Smith and Dick Rowe decide to sign another band of January auditionees, Brian Poole and the Tremeloes, and turn The Beatles down.

4 JANUARY
Mersey Beat prints the results of its first popularity poll, which is won handsomely by The Beatles.

5 JANUARY
To the relief of Brian Epstein, who's been trying to track down import copies of the single for Liverpudlian fans, 'My Bonnie' is released in Britain – with The Beatles credited under their own name for the first time.

12 FEBRUARY
The group auditions for the BBC in Manchester.

7 MARCH
The Beatles record their first radio session for the BBC, at the Corporation's Manchester studios. They tape three songs for transmission on the following day's edition of *Teenager's Turn*, with Lennon handling 'Memphis' and The Marvelettes' US R&B hit, 'Please Mr Postman'.

BBC recordings:
'Dream Baby', 'Memphis', 'Please Mr Postman'.

24 MARCH
Brian Epstein puts The Beatles into suits for the first time; ever afterwards, Lennon regards this jettisoning of their original leather gear as the first, and perhaps ultimate, sell-out of their career.

10 APRIL
In Hamburg, Stuart Sutcliffe dies of a brain haemorrhage in his girlfriend's arms.

11 APRIL
The Beatles fly from Manchester to Hamburg, where Stuart's girlfriend, photographer Astrid Kirchherr, greets them with the tragic news. Lennon affects the same outward insouciance he'd manufactured when his mother died. Astrid

Kirchherr: "He never cried. Not once. He went into this hysterical laughter, and couldn't stop. It was his way of not facing the truth. But he saved me. In his rough way, he was so beautiful, and he imposed his own method of recovery on me without me knowing it. 'Make up your mind, live or die', he would say. 'You're coming to the Star-Club with us tonight. Stop sitting at home – it won't bring Stu back.'"

13 APRIL - 31 MAY
The newly-opened Star-Club is The Beatles' home for the next six weeks.

23 APRIL
No-one tells The Beatles, but their 'My Bonnie' collaboration with Tony Sheridan is released in the States – with the 'Beat Brothers' once again getting the credit.

8/9 MAY
While his charges are overseas, Brian Epstein visits HMV House in London, and wangles a meeting with music publisher Sid Coleman. In turn, he arranges for Epstein to see Parlophone Records A&R manager George Martin the following day. Martin listens to a dub of the Decca audition thoughtfully, and agrees to audition the group, with a view to signing them to the label. Epstein cables his 'boys' in Hamburg: "Congratulations, boys. EMI request recording session. Please rehearse new material."

6 JUNE
The Beatles audition for Parlophone Records producers Ron Richards and George Martin at Abbey Road Studios in North London. The executives are impressed, eventually, after the group have run through a cover of The Coasters' R&B hit 'Besame Mucho', and three Lennon/McCartney originals, 'Love Me Do', 'P.S. I Love You' and 'Ask Me Why'. Only the last of these songs features a Lennon lead vocal, emphasising McCartney's dominance of The Beatles whenever they were trying to impress anyone over 30.

Soon after this initial session, George Martin offers to sign The Beatles to Parlophone, the least prestigious of the labels run by EMI.

11 JUNE
With their EMI contract confirmed, the group record their first BBC radio session in London, broadcast later this week on *Here We Go*.

BBC recordings:
'Ask Me Why', 'Besame Mucho', 'A Picture Of You'.

21 JUNE
The Beatles appear second on the bill to 'Hey Baby' hitmaker Bruce Channel at the Tower Ballroom in New Brighton. Backstage, Lennon strikes up a friendship with Channel's harmonica-player, Delbert McClinton, who in turn passes on some handy hints. Lennon's harmonica plays an important part in The Beatles' sound for the next two years and beyond.

16 AUGUST
Drummer Pete Best is sacked by The Beatles, ostensibly because George Martin has already told Brian Epstein that he is not proficient enough for recording sessions. But the dismissal is merely the culmination of an increasing rift between Best and the other three Beatles. In his place, Ringo Starr is recruited from rival Merseybeat band Rory Storm & the Hurricanes.

MID-AUGUST
Cynthia Powell discovers that she is pregnant. Lennon's reaction is immediate, if not entirely enthusiastic: the couple will have to get married.

22 AUGUST
A Granada TV crew films The Beatles at the Cavern, performing two versions of 'Some Other Guy' plus 'Kansas City'. It's the earliest existing film of the group in action. "We'll have to do that again," Lennon says sardonically after the first take.

23 AUGUST
John Winston Lennon and Cynthia Powell are married at Mount Pleasant Register Office

11

Below: **The Beatles at The Cavern.**
Centre: **John and Cynthia.**

25 OCTOBER
The group's first BBC session with Ringo produces three songs for *Here We Go*.

BBC recordings:
'Love Me Do', 'A Taste Of Honey', 'P.S. I Love You'.

LATE OCTOBER
In the knowledge that John will be away for much of November and December, Mimi Smith invites Cynthia to move in with her at 'Mendips' – and takes every opportunity to voice her disapproval of the circumstances of their marriage.

in Liverpool. The wedding lunch takes place at the same local restaurant where Lennon's parents celebrated their marriage in 1938.

That evening, the happy couple celebrate in style – or not, as The Beatles have a gig at the Riverpark Ballroom in Chester. The group enjoy only one evening off between now and September 17, setting the style for much of the Lennons' married life. Indeed, for the remainder of the year The Beatles continue to perform almost every night when they are in Liverpool.

John Lennon: "I went in the day before to tell Mimi. I said Cyn was having a baby, we were getting married tomorrow, did she want to come? She just let out a groan. There was a drill going on all the time outside the Register Office. I couldn't hear a word the bloke was saying. Then we went across the road and had a chicken dinner. It was all a laugh."

Today's edition of *Mersey Beat* includes a tasteful Lennon prose piece called 'Small Sam', which typifies his sense of humour by gaining as much mileage as possible from the club foot of its hero.

4 SEPTEMBER
With their new drummer in place, as George Martin has requested, The Beatles arrive at Abbey Road to record their first single. Martin has already procured 'How Do You Do It' from an outside writer, Mitch Murray, and insists that The

Beatles record it, with Lennon on uncharacteristically twee lead vocal. But they also tape one of their own songs, 'Love Me Do', and leave Martin in no doubt as to which they prefer.

Studio recordings:
'Love Me Do', 'How Do You Do It'.

6 SEPTEMBER
Lennon's literary exploits continue with the publication in *Mersey Beat* of another prose piece, 'On Safairy With Whide Hunter'.

11 SEPTEMBER
George Martin recalls The Beatles to Abbey Road, where he has lined up session drummer Andy White to take the place of Ringo Starr, who was understandably nervous and hence a little erratic a week earlier.

With his assistant Ron Richards actually supervising the session, the group recut 'Love Me Do' with White, record McCartney's 'P.S. I Love You', and then tentatively run through a Lennon original, 'Please Please Me', which is arranged like a Roy Orbison ballad.

The producer selects 'Love Me Do' as their début single, and Martin suggests that 'Please Please Me' shows promise, but needs substantially rearranging if it is to become a possible single.

Studio recordings:
'P.S. I Love You', 'Love Me Do', 'Please Please Me'.

5 OCTOBER
'Love Me Do'/'P.S. I Love You' is released by Parlophone as the group's first UK single in their own right. The publicity hand-out for the group lists Lennon's dislikes as "thick heads and traditional jazz", and his ambitions as "money and everything".

12 OCTOBER
The trade paper *Record Retailer* shows 'Love Me Do' as the 49th best-selling single in the country. It will eventually reach No. 17 in the chart, more than two months later.

17 OCTOBER
The Beatles make their live TV début , singing 'Love Me Do' on Granada's *People And Places*.

1-14 NOVEMBER
Another two-week stint for The Beatles at the Star-Club in Hamburg.

26 NOVEMBER
Back at Abbey Road, 'Please Please Me' has been rearranged to the satisfaction of George Martin, and is recorded with Lennon on lead vocals and harmonica. His 'Ask Me Why' is selected as the flipside of their next single. The group also attempt another dire Lennon/McCartney original.

While 'Love Me Do' has revealed little of The Beatles' promise, 'Please Please Me' is a clear signpost to the future, merging the melodicism of Buddy Holly and The Everly Brothers with the thrilling rush of the best rock'n'roll.

27 NOVEMBER
Still in London, it's time for The Beatles to tape a session for BBC Radio's *The Talent Spot*, which gives the nation its first chance to hear Lennon's raucous version of The Isley Brothers' hit, 'Twist And Shout'.

BBC recordings:
'Love Me Do', 'P.S. I Love You', 'Twist And Shout'.

3 DECEMBER
Another TV date to cash in on the hit single, as The Beatles appear on *Discs-A-Go-Go*.

4 DECEMBER
Tuesday Rendezvous is the group's latest TV booking.

15 DECEMBER
The Beatles top the bill at the *Mersey Beat* pollwinners' concert.

17 DECEMBER
A return visit to Granada TV's *People And Places*, to celebrate the continued sales of 'Love Me Do'.

18-31 DECEMBER
For the last time, The Beatles perform at the Star-Club in Hamburg. Their final show is recorded for posterity by Ted Taylor, alias Kingsize Taylor of the Dominoes, and is released on a double-LP 15 years later. Despite their obvious lack of enthusiasm for their surroundings, the tape does capture some of The Beatles' raw magic during their Hamburg performances, and showcases Lennon's ready, satirical wit, as well as his command of American rock'n'roll styles.

1963

1 JANUARY
At the end of their final stint in Hamburg's clubland, The Beatles fly back to London.

2 JANUARY
The Beatles are due to open a five-show tour of Scotland at the Longmore Hall in Leith, but the concert is cancelled when their flight is redirected from Edinburgh to Aberdeen.

Lennon briefly returns home to Liverpool to be with Cynthia.

3 JANUARY
The Scottish tour begins, with Lennon back in the ranks, at the Two Red Shoes Ballroom in Elgin.

4 JANUARY
Dingwall Town Hall is the night's prestigious venue.
   In the *NME*'s survey of 1962's most successful chart acts, The Beatles finish a commanding 111th.

5 JANUARY
The Beatles, billed as 'The Love Me Do Boys', play a show at the Museum Hall in Bridge of Allan.

6 JANUARY
The Beach Ballroom in Aberdeen is the last, and most prestigious, venue of the Scottish tour.

8 JANUARY
Three days before the release of 'Please Please Me', The Beatles mime the song on Scottish TV's *Roundup* in Glasgow.

10 JANUARY
Back to Liverpool for a show at the Grafton Rooms.

11 JANUARY
The 'Please Please Me' single is released. "I can't think of any other group currently recording in this style," notes *NME* reviewer and DJ, Keith Fordyce. "I shan't be in the least surprised to see the charts invaded by Beatles."
   After a lunchtime show at the Cavern, The Beatles drive to Old Hill in Staffordshire for a gig at the Plaza.

12 JANUARY
An early venture south of the Thames, to the Invicta Ballroom in Chatham, Kent.

13 JANUARY
The Beatles film their first appearance for ABC TV's *Thank Your Lucky Stars* in Birmingham, once again miming to 'Please Please Me'.

14 JANUARY
Ellesmere Port Civic Hall hosts The Beatles.

John Lennon: "I went in the day before to tell Mimi. I said Cyn was having a baby, we were getting married tomorrow, did she want to come? She just let out a groan. There was a drill going on all the time outside the Register Office. I couldn't hear a word the bloke was saying. Then we went across the road and had a chicken dinner. It was all a laugh."

16 JANUARY
The Beatles mime on Granada TV's live magazine show, *People And Places*, then tape a BBC radio show in the *Here We Go* series.

BBC recordings:
'Chains', 'Please Please Me', 'Three Cool Cats', 'Ask Me Why'.

17 JANUARY
The Cavern at lunchtime; the Majestic Ballroom in Birkenhead at night, where 500 fans are turned away at the door.

18 JANUARY
Another show, at the Floral Hall in Morecambe.

19 JANUARY
The *Thank Your Lucky Stars* show is aired, featuring The Beatles miming to 'Please Please Me'. That night, they perform at the Dodington Town Hall.

20 JANUARY
Night-time was the right time for The Beatles at the Cavern.

21 JANUARY
More miming for Radio Luxembourg, at EMI's HQ in London, for another show in *The Friday Spectacular* series.
   The Vee Jay label agrees to sign up The Beatles for the USA, and to issue 'Please Please Me' as their first American single.

22 JANUARY
A BBC triple-header for The Beatles in London, as they appear live on *Pop Inn*, and record episodes of *Saturday Club* and *The Talent Spot*.

BBC recordings:
'Some Other Guy', 'Love Me Do', 'Please Please Me', 'Keep Your Hands Off My Baby', 'Beautiful Dreamer', 'Please Please Me', 'Ask Me Why', 'Some Other Guy'.

23 JANUARY
Back to the Cavern Club for another evening show, after an eventful journey back to Liverpool, during which their van's windscreen shattered.

24 JANUARY
An in-store appearance in Liverpool to plug 'Please Please Me', and then a show at the Mold Assembly Hall in Wales.

25 JANUARY
'The Greatest Teenage Dance' at the Darwen Co-Op Hall sees The Beatles topping the bill over hopefuls like The Electones and The Mustangs.

26 JANUARY
Two evening shows, at the Macclesfield El Rio Club, and the Stoke King's Hall.

27 JANUARY
Another night, another show, this time at the Three Coins Club in Manchester. Lennon and McCartney (though mostly Lennon) write 'Misery' as a proposed single for Helen Shapiro.

28 JANUARY
The Majestic Ballroom in Newcastle stages a Beatles show.

30 JANUARY
The Cavern at lunchtime.

31 JANUARY
A repeat booking at the Cavern, with a return to the Majestic in Birkenhead that evening. Future TV star Freddie Starr is second on the bill, as they play two separate shows – proof of The Beatles' rapidly increasing popularity, and publicised as a first for any British ballroom.

1 FEBRUARY
Two evening shows, at the Assembly Rooms in Tamworth and then in Sutton Coldfield.

The word 'Beatles' appears for the first time on the cover of a national pop magazine, as the *New Musical Express* run an interview with the group. Writer Alan Smith notes their "clipped Negro sound", while Lennon admits that their latest single was a deliberate compromise: "We tried to make it as simple as possible. Some of the stuff we've written in the past has been a bit way-out, but we aimed this one straight at the hit parade."

2 FEBRUARY
The big time, at last – or at least the Gaumont in Bradford, on the first night of The Beatles' début national tour. 'Walking Back To Happiness' hitmaker Helen Shapiro tops the bill. Befitting their current chart status, The Beatles close the first half of the show. "They almost stole the show," comments one reviewer, "for the audience repeatedly called for them while other artists were performing."

3 FEBRUARY
After one night, the tour rests for two, allowing The Beatles to return to the Cavern.

The group are booked as co-headliners with Duane Eddy of their own tour, to begin in May. Meanwhile, EMI announce plans to tape the group at the Cavern Club for a live album.

4 FEBRUARY
Another Cavern show.

5 FEBRUARY
Back with Shapiro, The Beatles perform at the Doncaster Gaumont.

6 FEBRUARY
Another cinema, this time the Granada in Bedford, hosts the Shapiro/Beatles tour.

7 FEBRUARY
Back to Yorkshire, for a show at the Wakefield Regal.

8 FEBRUARY
The Carlisle ABC is the tour's latest stop. After the show, Ringo Starr is refused entry to a local golf club dance because of his unruly leather jacket, and Helen Shapiro and the rest of the group stomp off in sympathy. The incident brings The Beatles their first real national press coverage, albeit as bit players in a Helen Shapiro story.

9 FEBRUARY
The Empire Theatre in Sunderland stages tonight's show, after which the tour rests for two weeks.

11 FEBRUARY
One of the most momentous days in pop history, as The Beatles spend more than 12 hours at Abbey Road studios. During three separate sessions that day, they manage to record the outstanding ten songs for their first album, plus one tune ('Hold Me Tight') which is abandoned as being sub-standard.

Lennon begins the sessions with a heavy head-cold, nursed during the increasingly frantic touring schedule of recent weeks, and the resultant nasal quality to his voice is apparent on several tracks. But he still dominates the proceedings, leading the group through two deceptively self-revelatory compositions, 'Misery' and 'There's A Place', and two effortlessly soulful cover versions, Arthur Alexander's 'Anna' and The Shirelles' 'Baby It's You'.

The gem from this day's work, though, is the final act: John's tonsil-shredding rendition of The Isley Brothers' hit, 'Twist And Shout'. The first take is so intense that the second is little more than a mime-show. You can hear the toll it took on Lennon's voice every time you play the 'Please Please Me' LP.

Studio recordings:
'There's A Place', 'I Saw Her Standing There', 'A Taste Of Honey', 'Do You Want To Know A Secret', 'Misery', 'Hold Me Tight', 'Anna', 'Boys', 'Chains', 'Baby It's You', 'Twist And Shout'.

John Lennon: "My voice wasn't the same for a long time after. Every time I swallowed it was like sandpaper. We sang for 12 hours, almost non-stop. We had colds and we were concerned how it would affect the record. And by the end of the day, all we wanted to do was drink pints of milk."

12 FEBRUARY
Despite Lennon's cold and the prospect of another leg of the Shapiro tour later in the month, The Beatles continued their punishing nightly schedule – performing at the Azena in Sheffield, and then the Oldham Astoria.

13 FEBRUARY
The Hull Majestic stages another Beatles one-nighter.

14 FEBRUARY
Home to Liverpool for a gig at the Locarno Ballroom.

15 FEBRUARY
South to the Ritz Ballroom in Birmingham.

The *NME* prints The Beatles' 'lifelines'. John lists his personal ambition as "to write a musical", his professional as "to be rich and famous". He likes "blondes, leather" (an intriguing combination) and dislikes "stupid people".

16 FEBRUARY
South again, this time to the Carfax in Oxford.

17 FEBRUARY
In London, The Beatles mime to 'Please Please Me' during the taping of another show of TV's *Thank Your Lucky Stars*. At least their voices were rested for the night.

18 FEBRUARY
Back on the road, the "famous, fabulous, fantastic, sensational, magnificent, superb" Beatles top the bill at the Queens Hall in Widnes.

19 FEBRUARY
The Beatles look carefully in the other direction as Pete Best's latest band, Lee Curtis & The All Stars, support them at the Cavern Club.

20 FEBRUARY
Overnight, the group drive south to London, for a live appearance on BBC radio's *Parade Of The Pops*. They are then whisked back to Yorkshire for a show in Doncaster.

BBC recordings:
'Love Me Do', 'Please Please Me'.

21 FEBRUARY
Back on Merseyside, they headline two shows at the Majestic in Birkenhead.

22 FEBRUARY
Northern Songs, the company founded to publish The Beatles' songs, is officially incorporated. Dick James and Brian Epstein are named as the co-directors, with Lennon owning 19 of the 98 shares, McCartney one more than him.

That night, they invade Manchester's beat bastion, the Oasis.

'Please Please Me' ties with Frank Ifield's 'The Wayward Wind' at the No. 1 position in Britain's most prestigious pop chart, in the *New Musical Express*. The single subsequently tops the chart in its own right.

Lennon: "What made it more exciting was that we almost threw the song away as the B-side of 'Love Me Do'. We changed our minds only because we were so tired when we were recording it that we couldn't seem to get it right, and George Martin suggested we do another song instead."

23 FEBRUARY
After a fortnight of constant one-nighters, it's back to the Helen Shapiro tour, at the Mansfield Granada.

24 FEBRUARY
Coventry plays host to Shapiro and The Beatles.

25 FEBRUARY
Officially a night off from the tour, but Brian Epstein cancels their rest in favour of a gig at the Casino Ballroom in Leigh.

'Please Please Me' is released by Vee Jay, The Beatles' first US single in their own right.

26 FEBRUARY
The Beatles' tour regroups at the Taunton Gaumont.

27 FEBRUARY
The tour bus heads back north for a show at the York Rialto.

28 FEBRUARY
On the bus to their next show at the Shrewsbury Granada, Lennon and McCartney casually toss off another potential chart-topper, 'From Me To You'. A week later, though, Lennon tells an interviewer: "Our next single hasn't been written yet."

John Lennon: "We'd already written 'Thank You Girl' as the follow-up to 'Please Please Me'. This new number was to be the B-side. We were just fooling about on the guitar. Then we began to get a really good melody line and we started to work at it. Before that journey was over, we'd completed the lyric and everything. We were so pleased that we knew we had to make it the A-side."

1 MARCH
The Southport Odeon is the tour's next stop.

2 MARCH
Next on the schedule is the Sheffield City Hall.

3 MARCH
The Helen Shapiro tour ends in the auspicious surroundings of the Gaumont in Hanley.

4 MARCH
Another one-nighter, this time at the St. Helens Plaza.

5 MARCH
Having driven down from Lancashire overnight, The Beatles arrive in London in time for a photo-shoot at EMI House in Manchester Square, and then a 2.30pm session at Abbey Road with producer George Martin. Three songs are cut, with 'From Me To You' and 'Thank You Girl' selected in advance as the group's next single. To fill in time, John leads the group through several takes of one of his earliest compositions, 'The One After 909'; these remain unissued.

Studio recordings:
'From Me To You', 'Thank You Girl', 'The One After 909'.

15

6 MARCH

The Beatles' tape their fifth appearance on BBC radio's *Here We Go* pop show.

BBC recordings:
'Misery', 'Do You Want To Know A Secret', 'Please Please Me'.

7 MARCH

Billed as 'The Big Beatle Show', the group top the bill over Brian Epstein stablemates Gerry & the Pacemakers and Billy J. Kramer & the Dakotas at the Elizabethan Ballroom in Nottingham.

8 MARCH

The Ripon Hall in Harrogate makes sure The Beatles don't get a night off.

9 MARCH

The group's second tour begins at the East Ham Granada in East London. The Beatles are initially booked as third on the bill, behind visiting American stars Tommy 'Sheila' Roe and Chris 'Let's Dance' Montez.

After the first performance of the tour, however, it becomes apparent to the promoters that The Beatles were by far the most popular act on the bill. From the second house at East Ham onwards, they close the show.

10 MARCH

North to the Birmingham Hippodrome.

11 MARCH

The group's first non-performing day for a month.

12 MARCH

Lennon is forced to miss the show at the Bedford Granada because of flu.

John Lennon: "It's quite a strain, singing numbers like 'Twist And Shout' night after night. I lose my voice for days on end sometimes. Thankfully, it doesn't affect our act. We've got such a big repertoire of songs, we just arrange it so that the others fill in."

13 MARCH

Too ill to sing, Lennon can still play harmonica, which he does at Abbey Road, adding an overdub to 'From Me To You'. Back on the road, George and

Paul carry The Beatles' banner in York while Lennon remains in the wings.

14 MARCH

Three-man Beatles again, this time in Wolverhampton.

15 MARCH

Lennon rejoins the tour at the Colston Hall, Bristol.

16 MARCH

The group drive to London to perform live on BBC Radio's *Saturday Club*, before heading for their evening shows at the City Hall, Sheffield.

BBC recordings:
'I Saw Her Standing There', 'Misery', 'Too Much Monkey Business', 'I'm Talking About You', 'Please Please Me', 'Hippy Hippy Shake'.

17 MARCH

Next stop the Peterborough Embassy.

18 MARCH

The Gloucester Regal is their next port of call.

19 MARCH

Another Regal cinema awaits The Beatles, this time in Cambridge.

20 MARCH

The Romford ABC hosts the tour.

21 MARCH

Back to London in the morning for a BBC radio recording, as part of the *On The Scene* series, before shows at the Croydon ABC.

BBC recordings:
'Misery', 'Do You Want To Know A Secret', 'Please Please Me'.

22 MARCH

'Please Please Me', The Beatles' début album, is released by Parlophone.

Meanwhile, the group travel to Doncaster for tour dates at the Gaumont.

23 MARCH

Further North, to Newcastle City Hall.

24 MARCH

And then back home, to the Liverpool Empire.

25 MARCH

Taking advantage of their brief time in Liverpool, photographer Dezo Hoffmann shoots a session with the group in the city – from which come the famous 'bombsite' pictures used on the cover of the 'Twist & Shout' EP.

26 MARCH

Mansfield Granada hosts The Beatles.

27 MARCH

Two more shows, at Northampton ABC.

28 MARCH

A pioneering visit to the Exeter ABC.

29 MARCH

Lewisham Odeon in South-East London stages the next shows of the tour.

30 MARCH

Off to the Portsmouth Guildhall.

31 MARCH

Three weeks of constant travel ends at the De Montfort Hall in Leicester.

1 APRIL

Invited to co-host several BBC radio shows, titled *Side By Side*, with pop singer Karl Denver, The Beatles tape the first two programmes – the second not broadcast for another six weeks.

BBC recordings:
'Side By Side', 'I Saw Her Standing There', 'Do You Want To Know A Secret', 'Baby It's You', 'Please Please Me', 'From Me To You', 'Misery', 'From Me To You' (again), 'Long Tall Sally', 'A Taste Of Honey', 'Chains', 'Thank You Girl', 'Boys'.

3 APRIL

Back once again at the BBC, The Beatles tape a session for the weekly show *Easy Beat*.

BBC recordings:
'Please Please Me', 'Misery', 'From Me To You'.

4 APRIL

And the BBC again – this time for the third and last *Side By Side* taping.

BBC recordings:
'Too Much Monkey Business', 'Love Me Do', 'Boys', 'I'll Be On My Way', 'From Me To You'.

Liverpudlian schoolboy David Moores succeeds in booking The Beatles to appear at his public school, Stowe, in Buckinghamshire.

5 APRIL

At the Leyton Swimming Baths in East London, The Beatles receive a silver disc from EMI bigwigs, to celebrate 250,000 sales of 'Please Please Me'. After playing a quick set for their 'bosses', they go through the process again for a paying audience that night.

6 APRIL

The one-nighter circuit continues, as the group play the Buxton Pavilion.

7 APRIL

Back to Portsmouth eight days after their last show there, this time to appear at the Savoy Ballroom.

8 APRIL

Cynthia Lennon gives birth to a son, John Charles Julian, at Sefton General Hospital in Liverpool. Her husband is in London during the birth with the rest of The Beatles, leaving Cynthia with the formidable Aunt Mimi as her support. Equally terrifying is the knowledge that she must keep her relationship with John out of the public eye, for fear of damaging The Beatles' popularity. Even when John eventually visits her in hospital on April 10, she has to deny to her fellow patients that her husband is a member of The Beatles.

9 APRIL

Three separate engagements today: an interview for the BBC radio show *Pop Inn*, an appearance on ITV's *Tuesday Rendezvous*, and then an evening show at the Kilburn Ballroom in North London.

10 APRIL

Back to the familiar surroundings of the Majestic Ballroom in Birkenhead. Before the show, Lennon visits Cynthia at Sefton General Hospital, and sees his son for the first time.

the theatre via a secret rooftop entrance.

22-27 JULY
A second summer season, this time at the Weston-super-Mare Odeon.

22 JULY
Vee Jay Records of Chicago release the first US Beatles LP, 'Introducing The Beatles' – a slightly edited version of the 'Please Please Me' album.

26 JULY
Lennon's song 'Bad To Me' is released for the first time, by Billy J. Kramer with The Dakotas. On the flipside is another Lennon tune, 'I Call Your Name'.

28 JULY
Another show, at the Great Yarmouth ABC.

30 JULY
During a morning session at EMI, Lennon leads the group through 'Please Mr Postman', yet another masterful performance of a song from the Motown Records catalogue.

The group resist the temptation to repeat this gem when they adjourn to the BBC studios to tape a session for *Saturday Club*. Instead, they romp through the Carl Perkins favourite, 'Glad All Over'. They also tape an interview for the show *Non Stop Pop*.

Returning to Abbey Road in the evening, the group tape several more songs for their upcoming album.

Studio recordings:
'Please Mr Postman', 'It Won't Be Long', 'Money', 'Till There Was You', 'Roll Over Beethoven', 'All My Loving'.

BBC recordings:
'Long Tall Sally', 'She Loves You', 'Glad All Over', 'Twist And Shout', 'You Really Got A Hold On Me', 'I'll Get You'.

31 JULY
Driving back to Liverpool in the morning, the group perform once again at the Imperial Ballroom, Nelson.

1 AUGUST
Beat Monthly publisher Sean O'Mahony issues the first edition of *The Beatles Book*,

an authorised monthly publication devoted to The Beatles which appears regularly until December 1969. During the early years of publication, the group take a keen interest in the magazine's progress, though they eventually come to resent its endlessly cheerful and non-controversial reportage of their career.

It's *Pop Go The Beatles* time again, as the group tape another two episodes of the series. Lennon takes the lead vocal on Carl Perkins' 'Honey Don't', a song he passes on to Ringo the following year.

BBC recordings:
'Ooh! My Soul', 'Don't Ever Change', 'Twist And Shout', 'She Loves You', 'Anna', 'A Shot Of Rhythm And Blues', 'From Me To You', 'I'll Get You', 'Money', 'There's A Place', 'Honey Don't', 'Roll Over Beethoven', 'Baby It's You', 'Lucille', 'She Loves You'.

2 AUGUST
A farewell performance at the Grafton Rooms in Liverpool, a regular Beatles haunt over the previous 12 months.

3 AUGUST
For the final time, after something between 250 and 300 appearances, The Beatles headline the bill at the Cavern. Among the five support acts are Johnny Ringo and The Colts.

4 AUGUST
After a Sunday in Great Yarmouth, The Beatles returned to their usual Blackpool date, back at the Queen's Theatre.

5 AUGUST
Perhaps the only Beatles performance under canvas, as the group provide unlikely entertainment at the Urmston Show in Manchester.

6 AUGUST
For once, the group could fly, rather than drive, to their next venue, for two shows at the Springfield Ballroom on the Channel Island of Jersey.

7 AUGUST
A second night in Jersey. After the show, Lennon is invited to a "private party" on the island, which turns out to be a euphemism for an orgy. He

recounts his memories of the occasion five years later in the song 'Polythene Pam'.

8 AUGUST
And then on to Guernsey, at the Candie Auditorium.

Kyoko Cox, daughter of Anthony Cox and Yoko Ono, is born in Tokyo.

9 AUGUST
Back to the Springfield Ballroom in Jersey.

10 AUGUST
Final night at the Springfield, and The Beatles' last show in the Channel Islands.

11 AUGUST
If it's Sunday, it must be the Blackpool ABC. Earlier in the day, the group are greeted at Manchester Airport by their new road manager, Malcolm ('Mal') Evans, added to the group's team to assist Neil Aspinall.

12-17 AUGUST
Another week-long summer season begins, this time at the Llandudno Odeon.

13 AUGUST
'Twist And Shout' qualifies for a silver disc, thanks to 250,000 UK sales – the highest ever recorded for an extended-play release.

14 AUGUST
Before the night's show at Llandudno, they tape an appearance for Granada TV's *Scene At 6.30*.

18 AUGUST
The Beatles' car drives them to Birmingham, taping an appearance for ATV's *Lucky Stars (Summer Spin)*, on which they promote their next single, 'She Loves You'. That night, they perform at the Princess Theatre in Torquay.

19-24 AUGUST
Summer season No. 4, at the Bournemouth Gaumont.

23 AUGUST
'She Loves You' is released, selling 500,000 copies within two weeks.

25 AUGUST
Another trip to the Blackpool ABC for a Sunday night show.

26-31 AUGUST
The final weekly season of the summer, at the Southport Odeon.

27 AUGUST
The Beatles perform in front of BBC cameras, but no audience, at another Southport Theatre – footage used in the documentary *The Mersey Sound*. For the next few days, the Beeb's cameras track their progress around Liverpool.

30 AUGUST
Another group from Brian Epstein's stable, the Fourmost, become the first to release Lennon's song 'Hello Little Girl'.

1 SEPTEMBER
Their BBC obligations complete, The Beatles switch to the other side, to tape an appearance on ITV's *Big Night Out*.

3 SEPTEMBER
The group reconvene at the BBC studios to tape the final three shows in the *Pop Go The Beatles* series.

BBC recordings:
'Too Much Monkey Business', 'Till There Was You', 'Love Me Do', 'She Loves You', 'I'll Get You', 'The Hippy Hippy Shake', 'Chains', 'You Really Got A Hold On Me', 'Misery', 'Lucille', 'From Me To You', 'Boys', 'She Loves You', 'Ask Me Why', 'Devil In Her Heart', 'I Saw Her Standing There', 'Sure To Fall', 'Twist And Shout', 'A Taste Of Honey'.

4 SEPTEMBER
A run of one-nighters begins at the Worcester Gaumont.

5 SEPTEMBER
On to the Taunton Gaumont.

6 SEPTEMBER
And the Luton Odeon.

In the wake of the success of 'Twist And Shout', Parlophone issue an EP of 'The Beatles' Hits'.

below: The Beatles receiving gold discs from EMI chairman Sir Joseph Lockwood.

7 SEPTEMBER

Working well ahead, as ever, the group pre-record a session for the fifth birthday edition of BBC radio's *Saturday Club*, not due to be broadcast for another month. Lennon handles one of his Cavern Club staples, Chuck Berry's 'Memphis'.

BBC recordings:
'I Saw Her Standing There', 'Memphis, Tennessee', 'Happy Birthday', 'I'll Get You', 'She Loves You', 'Lucille'.

The run of concert dates ends at the Fairfield Hall in Croydon.

8 SEPTEMBER

Another summer comes to an end, as The Beatles play their last Sunday show at the Blackpool ABC.

10 SEPTEMBER

Former Beatles publicist turned Rolling Stones' manager, Andrew Oldham, meets The Beatles in the West End and invites them to attend a Stones rehearsal. Lennon and McCartney offer the band a new song, 'I Wanna Be Your Man', and retire to another room for a few minutes to knock off the missing middle section of the tune.

11 SEPTEMBER

Back at Abbey Road, the album sessions continue. Lennon introduces the soul ballad 'All I've Got To Do', and the intriguing, unsettling melody of 'Not A Second Time'.

Studio recordings:
'I Wanna Be Your Man', 'Little Child', 'All I've Got To Do', 'Not A Second Time', 'Don't Bother Me'.

12 SEPTEMBER

A second straight day of Abbey Road sessions.

Studio recordings:
'Hold Me Tight', 'Don't Bother Me', 'Little Child', 'I Wanna Be Your Man'.

13 SEPTEMBER

Back on the Lancashire ballroom circuit, with a gig at the Preston Public Hall.

14 SEPTEMBER

A return visit to the Northwich Memorial Hall.

15 SEPTEMBER

For the second time, The Beatles perform at the Royal Albert Hall in London – this time topping the bill of the Great Pop Prom.

16 SEPTEMBER

The Beatles break for a much-deserved holiday: this time Lennon opts to travel with his wife Cynthia, rather than Brian Epstein, spending two weeks in Paris. But Epstein comes along too.

'She Loves You' is released in the States, the group's first single on the Swan label. It reaches No. 1 more than five months later.

2 OCTOBER
John and Cynthia return to England.

3 OCTOBER
At EMI, the group add last-minute overdubs to their album tracks.

Studio recordings:
'I Wanna Be Your Man', 'Little Child'.

4 OCTOBER
The group mime to 'Twist And Shout', plus both sides of their latest single, on Rediffusion's *Ready Steady Go!*

5 OCTOBER
The year's second short tour of Scotland begins at the Glasgow Concert Hall.

6 OCTOBER
The Kirkcaldy Carlton is tonight's venue.

7 OCTOBER
The brief tour ends at the Caird Hall in Dundee.

9 OCTOBER
After a brief stop in Liverpool, The Beatles return to London on John Lennon's 23rd birthday to tape a song for later broadcast on radio's *The Ken Dodd Show*.

BBC recording:
'She Loves You'.

11 OCTOBER
A one-off show at the Trentham Ballroom.

12 OCTOBER
The Beatles rehearse for their first Palladium appearance at the London Fan Club HQ.

13 OCTOBER
More than 15,000,000 people tune in to ATV's *Sunday Night At The London Palladium*, to see The Beatles top the bill over Brook Benton and Des O'Connor on television's most popular light entertainment show. A few hundred fans cause some degree of chaos outside the venue.

14 OCTOBER
'Beatlemania' is born, as the London press seize on the previous night's 'disturbances', magnify them a few times, and suggest that central London has been under siege from hysterical fans. Thereafter, the hysteria is self-perpetuating. *Daily Herald*: "When The Beatles, with their bobbed haircuts, finished their 12-minute act, the trouble really started. Screaming girls launched themselves against the police – sending helmets flying and constables reeling. Police vans sealed off the front of the theatre so that The Beatles could be smuggled out. Stage-doorman George Cooper said: "There's been nothing like it since American singer Johnnie Ray came here in 1955."

15 OCTOBER
In theory, Beatlemania is relaxed for a night, as The Beatles return to the more familiar territory of the Floral Hall in Southport. But the show coincides with the announcement that the group have been invited to play at the Royal Command Performance in November, and the national press pursue The Beatles to the Lancashire coast.

16 OCTOBER
The group run gently through a familiar segment of their stage repertoire for BBC radio's *Easy Beat*.

BBC recordings:
'I Saw Her Standing There', 'Love Me Do', 'Please Please Me', 'From Me To You', 'She Loves You'.

17 OCTOBER
Using a four-track recording console for the first time, The Beatles record their next single, 'I Want To Hold Your Hand', and a special message which will be included on a single sent out to members of their Official Fan Club. Lennon uses the occasion to bastardise the words of 'Good King Wenceslas'. Besides co-writing the A-side of the single, Lennon also contributes the touching B-side ballad, 'This Boy'.

Studio recordings:
'The Beatles' Christmas Record', 'You Really Got A Hold On Me', 'I Want To Hold Your Hand', 'This Boy'.

19 OCTOBER
The Buxton Pavilion hosts The Beatles, accompanied by "screaming girls, struggling policeman, a constable's helmet rolling on the floor".

20 OCTOBER
Another *Thank Your Lucky Stars* performance is taped.

23 OCTOBER
That night, the group fly to Stockholm for their first overseas tour.

24 OCTOBER
The Swedish radio show *Pop '63* is graced by an appearance by The Beatles.

25 OCTOBER
Beatlemania is proved to have spread beyond British shores, as the group play two shows at a school in Karlstad, west of Stockholm.

26 OCTOBER
To the Swedish capital, for shows at the Kungliga Hall.

27 OCTOBER
A rare three-show day, at the Gothenberg Circus on the Swedish west coast.

28 OCTOBER
Returning slowly east, the Boras Hall stages its night of Beatles glory.

29 OCTOBER
The Sports Hall in Eskilstuna, close to Stockholm, hosts The Beatles. Back in London, Brian Epstein concludes his negotiations for the group to make their début feature film for United Artists in 1964.

Lennon: "After this film, they'll find out we're not actors and that will be that. We're going to race through it, and I'll probably lose all confidence by the time it's over. I mean, none of us are going to learn our lines. I just don't have the concentration. And we're not really capable of ad-libbing."

30 OCTOBER
A live Beatles performance is taped for the Swedish TV show *Drop In*.

31 OCTOBER
Back to London, to the first mass welcome from hundreds of screaming fans at Heathrow Airport – duly documented by press and TV cameras.

1 NOVEMBER
At last, The Beatles headline a British tour in their own right, opening the schedule with two shows at the Cheltenham Odeon. Also on the less-than-stellar bill are Peter Jay & The Jaywalkers, The Brook Brothers, The Kestrels and fellow Liverpudlians The Vernons Girls.

The Beatles' nightly set clocks in at about 25 minutes, and ten songs – climaxing with Lennon's tonsil-searing rendition of 'Twist And Shout'.

Parlophone pull an EP from their début album entitled 'The Beatles (No. 1)', with 'I Saw Her Standing There' as the lead track. On the same day, Billy J. Kramer releases another Lennon/McCartney tune for the first time, 'I'll Keep You Satisfied'; and The Rolling Stones' 'I Wanna Be Your Man', completed by John and Paul for the group in September, also reaches the shops.

2 NOVEMBER
Next stop — the Sheffield City Hall. Meanwhile, *The Daily Telegraph* runs an anguished leader comparing the hysteria of The Beatles' fans to Nazis at a Nuremburg rally.

3 NOVEMBER
And then the Leeds Odeon.

4 NOVEMBER
One of the most memorable concert appearances in Beatles history, as The Beatles play in front of the Queen Mother at the Prince Of Wales Theatre in London, as part of the Royal Command Performance (otherwise known as the Royal Variety Show). The group — low on the bill beneath international stars like Buddy Greco, Marlene Dietrich and Tommy Steele — perform four songs, 'She Loves You', 'Till There Was You', 'From Me To You' and 'Twist And Shout'. But the evening's most significant moment comes when Lennon introduces the final song: "For this number, we'd like to ask your help. Will the people in the cheaper seats clap your hands, and the rest of you, if you'll just rattle your jewellery." His quip ("I'll just ask them to rattle their fucking jewellery", he promises before the show) is regarded as a charming piece of working-class cheekiness, and does much to endear the group to the showbiz establishment and the adult population — particularly when the show is broadcast on TV a week later.
   Lennon: "We were news at the time, and it only just happened we clicked in 14 editors' minds at the same time. Then this photographer said a week or two later, 'We *made* them, you know'. I'd like to meet him and hear him say that to my face."

5 NOVEMBER
Back on tour, at the Slough Adelphi.
   After one day of orders, requests for 500,000 copies of the next single, 'I Want To Hold Your Hand', are reported to have been received by EMI.
   The *Daily Mirror* greets the group's Variety Show performance with an editorial headed: "Yeah! Yeah! Yeah!".

"They're young, new," the paper's leader-writer gasps, "They're high spirited, cheerful. What a change from the self-pitying moaners crooning their love-lorn tunes from the tortured shallows of lukewarm hearts. The Beatles are whacky. They wear their hair like a mop – but it's WASHED, it's super clean. So is their fresh young act. They don't have to rely on off-colour jokes about homos for their fun."

6 NOVEMBER
The Northampton ABC is the night's venue.

7 NOVEMBER
The British tour didn't preclude The Beatles' only performance in Ireland, at the Dublin Adelphi.

8 NOVEMBER
North to the Belfast Ritz.

9 NOVEMBER
Back to London, for a show at the East Ham Granada.

10 NOVEMBER
The Birmingham Hippodrome plays host to The Beatles.

11 NOVEMBER
In New York, Brian Epstein persuades eminent TV host Ed Sullivan to book The Beatles onto his show in February.

13 NOVEMBER
The Plymouth ABC stages The Beatles' latest show.

14 NOVEMBER
The group appear at the Exeter ABC.

15 NOVEMBER
Next stop is the Colston Hall, Bristol.
   The Fourmost release another previously unheard Lennon/McCartney tune, 'I'm In Love'. Lennon has written this nondescript beat ballad four months earlier, explicitly as a giveaway song.

16 NOVEMBER
As The Beatles perform at the Bournemouth Winter Gardens, several US TV teams choose this evening to check out the latest British showbiz sensation.

17 NOVEMBER
America drinks up and goes home; The Beatles play the Coventry Theatre.

18 NOVEMBER
EMI presents The Beatles with a couple of handfuls of gold and silver discs during a ceremony at the company's London HQ. After the event, Brian Epstein meets a South African tour promoter, but rejects his offer of a lucrative series of concerts to segregated audiences.

19 NOVEMBER
Back on the road, at the Wolverhampton Gaumont.

20 NOVEMBER
Watched by Pathé News cameras, who film several songs for the newsreel movie *The Beatles Come To Town*, the group perform at the Manchester ABC.

21 NOVEMBER
Another ABC cinema, this time in Carlisle.

22 NOVEMBER
On to the Stockton Globe.
   The 'With The Beatles' album is released by Parlophone, attracting as much attention for the half-shaded Robert Freeman cover photo as for the vibrant beat music on the record. Almost half a million copies are sold by the end of the year.

23 NOVEMBER
Followed by the more prestigious Newcastle City Hall.

24 NOVEMBER
The Hull ABC is The Beatles' latest venue.

26 NOVEMBER
South to the Cambridge Regal. "How long do you think the group will last?" a pressman asks Lennon backstage. "About five years," is his laconic reply.

27 NOVEMBER
After filming another appearance on *Scene At 6.30*, the group perform at the York Rialto. Backstage, the discussion turns to Dick Rowe, the Decca Records executive who rejected the group in 1962. "He must be kicking himself,"

McCartney reflects. Lennon replies: "I hope he kicks himself to death."

28 NOVEMBER
Lincoln ABC presents The Beatles.

29 NOVEMBER
This time it's the Huddersfield ABC.
   'I Want To Hold Your Hand' is released – advance orders having already topped one million in the UK alone.

30 NOVEMBER
The Empire Theatre in Sunderland hosts The Beatles.

1 DECEMBER
Leicester De Montfort Hall is tonight's venue.

2 DECEMBER
At the ATV studios north of London, The Beatles are guests during the filming of an episode of *The Morecambe And Wise Show*. "My father told me about you," Lennon tells Morecambe kindly.
   That evening, they perform at a benefit show at the Grosvenor House Hotel in London's Park Lane. "We were awful," Lennon notes after the show. "If anyone tells us we were good tonight I'll spit in their faces."

3 DECEMBER
They perform at the Portsmouth Guildhall.

7 DECEMBER
Three full concert shows and a TV filming during the same day: at the Liverpool Empire, The Beatles record an episode of BBC TV's *Juke Box Jury* for transmission that evening, filling all four places on the celebrity panel which judges new releases by artists like Elvis Presley and Billy Fury. Also broadcast by the BBC that night (under the title *It's The Beatles*) is the group's afternoon set at the Empire, in front of 2,500 members of their Official Fan Club.
   That night, The Beatles switch venues from the Empire to the Odeon, for the standard two shows of their UK tour.

8 DECEMBER
Lewisham Odeon in South London offers The Beatles no respite after the previous day's activities.

9 DECEMBER
Next stop: Southend Odeon.

10 DECEMBER
Doncaster Gaumont is the group's home for the night. During a radio interview that evening, Lennon recites one of his poems, 'Neville Club', and reveals that he is compiling a book of his writings.

11 DECEMBER
Up to the Scarborough Futurist Theatre.

12 DECEMBER
Their fourth UK tour of 1963 ends at the Southampton Gaumont.

14 DECEMBER
A week after the Liverpool Fan Club concert, The Beatles perform to their southern fans, at a Club Convention staged at the Wimbledon Palais. The group sit behind the venue's bar while all 3,000 concert-goers file past and shake their hands; then they perform, behind a special cage designed by the Palais management to protect their precious stage from Beatlemaniacs.

15 DECEMBER
Another TV taping, this time for the pre-Christmas *Thank Your Lucky Stars* – a chance to promote the latest single, 'I Want To Hold Your Hand'.

17 DECEMBER
In their first BBC radio session for two months, the group record another set for *Saturday Club*.

BBC recordings:
'All My Loving', 'This Boy', 'I Want To Hold Your Hand', 'Till There Was You', 'Roll Over Beethoven', 'She Loves You'

18 DECEMBER
Back at the BBC, the group tape a Boxing Day radio special, entitled *From Us To You* – concentrating on familiar songs

from their records, aside from the title tune (a revamp of 'From Me To You').

BBC recordings:
'From Us To You', 'She Loves You', 'All My Loving', 'Roll Over Beethoven', 'Till There Was You', 'Boys', 'Money', 'I Saw Her Standing There', 'I Want To Hold Your Hand'.

At the Prince Charles Theatre in London, a ballet called *Mods And Rockers*, performed by the Western Theatre company to the music of Lennon and McCartney, opens a month-long season.

20 DECEMBER
Granada TV's *Scene At 6.30*, a regular haunt for The Beatles in 1963, receives another visit.

21 DECEMBER
Steeped in showbiz and theatre tradition, Beatles manager Brian Epstein happily goes along with the conventions of early Sixties British pop by booking The Beatles a Christmas residency. Most top UK stars played pantomime over the festive season; The Beatles narrowly escape that fate, by agreeing to take the leading roles in their own Christmas Show.

By way of a rehearsal for the season of performances in London, The Beatles and their supporting cast – Billy J. Kramer & The Dakotas, Cilla Black, The Fourmost, The Barron Knights, Tommy Quickly and MC Rolf Harris – perform at the Bradford Gaumont. Obliged to hold the stage for ten minutes while The Beatles' equipment is set-up, Harris is drowned out by screaming girls.

22 DECEMBER
Another warm-up for the Christmas season, this time at the Liverpool Empire.

24, 26-28, 30-31 DECEMBER
The Beatles' Christmas Show, introduced by Rolf Harris and devised and produced by Peter Yolland, is staged at the Finsbury Park Astoria in North London, right through to 11 January.

The Beatles close the show with a nine-song performance, but also take part in some pleasantly inane seasonal sketches – the finer points of which (mostly pre-recorded) are submerged in the general

hysteria which greets their every appearance on stage.

After the first performance, the group are flown home to Liverpool for Christmas with their families.

26 DECEMBER
An early start for the flight back to London, and the continuation of the professional Christmas festivities.

In the States, Capitol Records release their first Beatles single – 'I Want To Hold Your Hand'.

27 DECEMBER
The Times names Lennon and McCartney the "outstanding English composers of 1963".

29 DECEMBER
The Sunday Times goes one step further than its sister paper; the two Beatles are "the greatest composers since Beethoven".

1964

1-4, 6-11 JANUARY
At the Finsbury Park Astoria, The Beatles play out their Christmas Show season to sell-out audiences.

7 JANUARY
They tape a *Saturday Club* session for the BBC, to be aired while they are in the States in February.

BBC recordings:
'All My Loving', 'Money', 'The Hippy Hippy Shake', 'I Want To Hold Your Hand', 'Roll Over Beethoven', 'Johnny B. Goode', 'I Wanna Be Your Man'.

12 JANUARY
For the second and last time, The Beatles perform on the live ITV show, *Sunday Night At The London Palladium*, alongside their friend, singer Alma Cogan.

14 JANUARY
The group fly to Paris to begin a lengthy series of concerts in France.

15 JANUARY
The Beatles play a warm-up show at the Cinema Cyrano in Versailles, preceded by a juggling act. Earlier, they stroll through the streets of Paris, virtually ignored by the local population.

Daily Mail: "Either the Champs-Elysées was not in mobbing mood today, or Beatlemania is still, like Britain's entry into the Common Market, a problem the French prefer to put off for a while. Exactly three girls asked them for autographs. One was English."

Back at their Paris hotel, they are informed that 'I Want To Hold Your Hand' has reached No. 1 in the US *Cashbox* charts after just three weeks in the Hot 100. Celebrations ensue.

16 JANUARY - 4 FEBRUARY
For almost three weeks, the group play an extended season of concerts – usually at least two per day – at the Olympia Theatre, a popular Parisian concert/cabaret venue. They're billed as co-stars alongside 'If I Had A Hammer' hitmaker Trini Lopez, and French chanteuse Sylvie Vartan. In front of a predominantly male audience – a complete contrast to what they're used to in Britain – The Beatles struggle to match their advance publicity, and to cope with repeated equipment failure, and the British (and French) press is quick to capitalise on their 'failure'. During the first show, Lennon recites the only line of French he knows: "Je me lève à sept heures". "How barbaric", responds a fan in the front row.

John escapes the post-show mêlee of journalists and photographers with *Daily Mail* reporter Maureen Cleave.

20 JANUARY
'Meet The Beatles!' screams the title of the group's second US LP, and their first on their new label, Capitol; within three weeks it is No. 1 in the charts. It is the first of a remarkable 33 Beatles records released in the States in 1964.

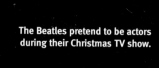

The Beatles pretend to be actors
during their Christmas TV show.

19 JULY
Another seaside Sunday show, this time at the Blackpool ABC – broadcast live on ABC TV's *Blackpool Night Out*.

20 JULY
A week after their last release, Capitol issue two further US Beatles singles, Lennon's 'I'll Cry Instead' (No. 25) and McCartney's 'And I Love Her' (No. 12). The label also issue the 'Something New' album, a ragbag of tracks from earlier UK releases which haven't been available in the States. It makes No. 2, behind 'A Hard Day's Night'.

23 JULY
The Beatles appear at the London Palladium for the last time, as part of a charity spectacular, *The Night Of A Hundred Stars*.

26 JULY
Back to Blackpool, for a concert at the town's Opera House.

28/29 JULY
Two days of shows at the Johanneshovs Isstadion in Stockholm, Sweden – their last concerts in Scandinavia. The group also appear on Swedish TV, allowing Lennon to recite his poem 'Good Dog Nigel' to baffled viewers.

2 AUGUST
The summer season continues, with a show at the Bournemouth Gaumont.

9 AUGUST
The Scarborough Futurist Theatre is the latest Sunday venue.

10 AUGUST
Capitol reissue four Beatles singles in the States: 'Do You Want To Know A Secret', 'Please Please Me', 'Love Me Do' and 'Twist And Shout'.

11 AUGUST
The Beatles return to Abbey Road, to tape a rare (by 1964) Lennon/McCartney collaboration, 'Baby's In Black'.

Studio recording:
'Baby's In Black'.

14 AUGUST
Another Abbey Road session documents Lennon's remarkable range. 'I'm A Loser' reflects his fascination with the music of Bob Dylan, while its lyrics extend the theme of an earlier 1964 composition, 'I'll Cry Instead'. The cover of the Johnny Preston hit 'Leave My Kitten Alone' is perhaps the fiercest of all The Beatles' rock'n'roll covers, but despite that, it is not released.

Studio recordings:
'I'm A Loser', 'Mr Moonlight', 'Leave My Kitten Alone'.

16 AUGUST
The last UK Beatles show of the summer, back at the Blackpool Opera House.

17 AUGUST
Lennon gives designer Ken Partridge free rein to revamp the interior of his Weybridge home, against the wishes of his wife Cynthia. Work continues for months, during which time the Lennons are virtually imprisoned in a small corner of the mansion.

18 AUGUST
The group fly out of London en route to California, via Winnipeg. On arrival in San Francisco, they narrowly escape injury during hysterical scenes at the airport. That night, Lennon, Ringo Starr and the group's press officer, Derek Taylor, visit a nightclub run by organ-player Billy Preston.

19 AUGUST
Their first full-scale US tour begins at the Cow Palace in San Francisco. The group's support bands on this tour include the Bill Black Combo, The Exciters and The Righteous Brothers.

20 AUGUST
Two shows at the Las Vegas Convention Center – the second performed under the shadow of a telephoned bomb scare.

21 AUGUST
Next stop: the Seattle Coliseum.

22 AUGUST
The Beatles' first show in Canada, at the Empire Stadium in Vancouver.

23 AUGUST
Capitol Records engineers tape The Beatles' performance at the Hollywood Bowl.

24 AUGUST
To compensate for the non-release in the States of the 'Long Tall Sally' EP, Capitol issue two tracks from that record as a single, 'Matchbox'/'Slow Down'. It reaches No. 17.

26 AUGUST
Twenty years before U2 immortalise the venue, The Beatles perform at the Red Rocks Amphitheater near Denver.

27 AUGUST
Concert at the Cincinnati Gardens. Cincinnati journalist: "What will you do when Beatlemania is over?" Lennon: "Count our money." Journalist: "Surely you don't need the protection of the police? Can't you handle your fans by yourselves?" Lennon: "Well, maybe you could. You're fatter than we are."

28/29 AUGUST
Two shows at Forest Hills Stadium in New York. At the Delmonico Hotel after the first concert, The Beatles meet Bob Dylan, who introduces them to the smoky charms of marijuana cigarettes.

30 AUGUST
The Beatles move on to the Atlantic City Convention Hall.

2 SEPTEMBER
Concert at the Philadelphia Convention Hall.

3 SEPTEMBER
The Beatles venture into the State Fair circuit, playing the Indiana event in Indianapolis.

4 SEPTEMBER
On to the Milwaukee Arena.

5 SEPTEMBER
And then to the International Amphitheater in Chicago.

> *Cincinnati journalist:* "What will you do when Beatlemania is over?"
> *Lennon:* "Count our money."
> *Journalist:* "Surely you don't need the protection of the police? Can't you handle your fans by yourselves?"
> *Lennon:* "Well, maybe you could. You're fatter than we are."

6 SEPTEMBER
More shows, this time at the Olympia Stadium in Detroit.

7 SEPTEMBER
Back to Canada, for concerts at the Maple Leaf Gardens in Toronto.

8 SEPTEMBER
The Montreal Forum hosts The Beatles.

9-10 SEPTEMBER
Two days of relaxation in Key West, Florida.

11 SEPTEMBER
The group brave a nearby hurricane to perform at the largest venue of their '64 tour, The Gator Bowl in Jacksonville.

12 SEPTEMBER
Out of the reach of Hurricane Dora, and on to the Boston Garden.

13 SEPTEMBER
Two shows at the Baltimore Civic Center.

14 SEPTEMBER
Next stop: the Pittsburgh Civic Arena.

15 SEPTEMBER
The performance at the Cleveland Public Auditorium is halted by police after fans invade the stage.

16 SEPTEMBER
South to the City Park Stadium in New Orleans.

17 SEPTEMBER
The Beatles celebrate their visit to the Municipal Stadium at Kansas City by opening their set with their R&B song named after the town.

18 SEPTEMBER
On to the Memorial Auditorium in Dallas.

19 SEPTEMBER
The charity Oxfam print hundreds of thousands of copies of a Christmas card featuring a specially commissioned John Lennon drawing.

20 SEPTEMBER
An epic month of almost non-stop air travel brings The Beatles back to New York, for a

charity show at the Paramount Theater. Afterwards, the group relax at their hotel with Bob Dylan, and Lennon does his best to avoid being interviewed by journalist Gloria Steinem.

21 SEPTEMBER
Home to London.

29-30 SEPTEMBER
Maintaining his dominance of the group's 1964 recording sessions, Lennon introduces three effortlessly strong songs at Abbey Road, 'Every Little Thing', 'No Reply' and 'I Don't Want To Spoil The Party'. They reveal his mastery of his craft, though craftsmanship is no longer enough for his own satisfaction.

Studio recordings:
'Every Little Thing', 'I Don't Want To Spoil The Party', 'What You're Doing', 'No Reply'.

1 OCTOBER
Vee Jay in the States achieve new heights of imaginative marketing, by reissuing their 'Introducing The Beatles' LP as part of a double-album set, 'The Beatles Vs. The Four Seasons'. But the public are cottoning on to the cash-ins, and the set peaks at No. 142.

2/3 OCTOBER
The Beatles tape three songs for broadcast on the US TV show *Shindig*. Among them is

Lennon's 'I'm A Loser', being performed in front of an audience for the first time.

5 OCTOBER
Yet another Beatles LP hits American stores: 'Ain't She Sweet'.

6 OCTOBER
While Lennon toys with the Bobby Parker-inspired riff for his new song, 'I Feel Fine', between takes, the group record another track for their forthcoming album.

Studio recordings:
'Eight Days A Week'.

8 OCTOBER
Another Abbey Road session, to cut the B-side of their next single.

Studio recordings:
'She's A Woman'.

9 OCTOBER
The Beatles' first UK tour for almost a year opens on Lennon's 24th birthday at the Bradford Gaumont. The group are supported by Mary Wells, Sounds Incorporated, Tommy Quickly, Michael Haslam and The Rustiks.

10 OCTOBER
Concert at Leicester De Montfort Hall.

35

36

11 OCTOBER
Birmingham Odeon.

12 OCTOBER
More Stateside repackaging, as Vee Jay concoct the 'Songs, Pictures And Stories Of The Fabulous Beatles' LP for the US market. It makes No. 63, despite repeating the same basic set of tracks as all the other Vee Jay LPs.

13 OCTOBER
Wigan ABC.

14 OCTOBER
Another appearance on that Granada TV favourite, *Scene At 6.30*, before a show at the Manchester ABC.

15 OCTOBER
Stockton Globe.

16 OCTOBER
Hull ABC.

18 OCTOBER
A mini-revolution at Abbey Road, as Lennon introduces deliberate amplifier feedback to the recording of popular music, as an introduction to 'I Feel Fine'. He also storms through a single majestic take of Chuck Berry's 'Rock And Roll Music'.

Studio recordings:
'Eight Days A Week', 'Kansas City', 'Mr Moonlight', 'I Feel Fine', 'I'll Follow The Sun', 'Everybody's Trying To Be My Baby', 'Rock And Roll Music', 'Words Of Love'.

19 OCTOBER
Back on the road, at the Edinburgh ABC.

20 OCTOBER
The Caird Hall, Dundee.

21 OCTOBER
Glasgow Odeon.

22 OCTOBER
Another Odeon concert, this time in Leeds.

23 OCTOBER
The Kilburn Gaumont.

24 OCTOBER
Another London show, at the Walthamstow Granada.

25 OCTOBER
The Beatles win five Ivor Novello Awards, at the British music business's annual celebration of itself. Among their prizes: 'Most Outstanding Contribution To Music In 1963'.

26 OCTOBER
The 'Beatles For Sale' album is completed during a break in the tour, while the group also tape their second annual message to their Fan Club members.

Studio recordings:
'Honey Don't', 'What You're Doing', 'Another Beatles Christmas Record'.

29 OCTOBER
The tour resumes at the Plymouth ABC.

30 OCTOBER
Bournemouth Gaumont.

31 OCTOBER
Ipswich Gaumont.

1 NOVEMBER
Back to London, and the Finsbury Park Astoria.

2 NOVEMBER
The Beatles' second – and last – Northern Ireland concert, at the Belfast King's Hall.

4 NOVEMBER
Luton Ritz.

5 NOVEMBER
Nottingham Odeon.

6 NOVEMBER
Southampton Gaumont. Parlophone release two Beatles UK EPs, 'Extracts From The Film *A Hard Day's Night*', and 'Extracts From The Album A Hard Day's Night'.

7 NOVEMBER
Cardiff Capitol.

8 NOVEMBER
The group return home to the Liverpool Empire, where their concert is viewed by an audience of local luminaries. After the show, Lennon visits Stuart Sutcliffe's parents, who allow him to choose one of Stuart's paintings as a memento.

9 NOVEMBER
Sheffield City Hall.

10 NOVEMBER
The Beatles' penultimate UK tour ends at Bristol Colston Hall.

14 NOVEMBER
Another appearance on *Thank Your Lucky Stars* goes into the can.

16 NOVEMBER
Miming to 'I Feel Fine' and 'She's A Woman', The Beatles film clips are to be inserted in *Top Of The Pops* the following month.

17 NOVEMBER
The Beatles tape their final appearance on BBC Radio's *Top Gear*.

BBC recordings:
'I'm A Loser', 'Honey Don't', 'She's A Woman', 'Everybody's Trying To Be My Baby', 'I'll Follow The Sun', 'I Feel Fine'.

20 NOVEMBER
Lennon is a guest during the filming of an episode of Peter Cook and Dudley Moore's BBC 2 comedy series, *Not Only... But Also*. He takes part in sketches with the two comedians.

23 NOVEMBER
The group film their last appearance on *Ready, Steady, Go!* – miming to both sides of their new single and two LP songs, 'Kansas City' and 'Baby's In Black'.

'I Feel Fine' becomes Capitol's sixth US Beatles single this year. In a shock development, it takes almost a month to reach No. 1. The label also release 'The Beatles' Story', a 48-minute, two-LP documentary set which features interviews, inane narration and a few seconds of the group on

stage at the Hollywood Bowl in August. Expensive and exploitative, it still sells well enough to reach No. 7.

25 NOVEMBER
Another farewell, as the group tape a *Saturday Club* session for the last time.

BBC recordings:
'Rock And Roll Music', 'I'm A Loser', 'Everybody's Trying To Be My Baby', 'I Feel Fine', 'Kansas City', 'She's A Woman'.

27 NOVEMBER
'I Feel Fine' is released as The Beatles' final UK single of 1964.

28 NOVEMBER
John is interviewed at home by BBC radio, as part of the promotion for the 'Beatles For Sale' album.

29 NOVEMBER
Returning to the studio where Cook and Moore are taping *Not Only... But Also*, Lennon recites several of his poems, with help from the comedians and their sidekicks.

4 DECEMBER
'Beatles For Sale', its title, cover photo and contents betraying a certain world-weariness, is released in the UK

15 DECEMBER
Capitol Records in the States chop several tracks from the 'Beatles For Sale' album, add in the latest single, and release the result as 'Beatles '65'. It makes No. 1 within three weeks.

22 DECEMBER
In rehearsal for their Xmas show, The Beatles are interviewed for *Top Of The Pops*.

24, 26, 28-31 DECEMBER
The group star in Another Beatles Christmas Show, at the Hammersmith Odeon in West London. The 'spectacular' is as original as its title, with the group forced to endure some appallingly crass 'comedy' sketches, before performing a full live set in the second half. The show is hosted by DJ Jimmy Savile, and also features Freddie & The Dreamers, The Yardbirds, Ray Fell, Sounds Incorporated, Michael Haslam, Elkie Brooks and The Mike Cotton Sound.

1965

1-2, 4-9, 11-16 JANUARY
Another Beatles Christmas Show limps two weeks into the New Year. Once the season is complete, The Beatles vow never to take part in a similar exercise again.

9 JANUARY
The episode of *Not Only... But Also* featuring John Lennon is screened on BBC 2.

27 JANUARY
Another Beatles music publishing company is formed, with Lennon and McCartney appointed directors: Maclen Music Ltd.

1 FEBRUARY
The final US Beatles EP, '4 By The Beatles', is released.

11 FEBRUARY
John attends the wedding of Ringo Starr and Maureen Cox at Caxton Hall Register Office in London.

15-20 FEBRUARY
During a week of sessions at EMI, the group tape the songs for the *Help!* movie, and their next single. The dense rhythm guitar sound of Lennon's 'Ticket To Ride' is a definite nod in the direction of The Rolling Stones, while 'You've Got To Hide Your Love Away' is a self-conscious

attempt to ape Bob Dylan's confessional style. Elsewhere, though, both Lennon and McCartney are showing signs of lapsing into the ways of the hack songsmith, writing three-minute beat ballads to order.

Studio recordings:
'Ticket To Ride', 'Another Girl', 'I Need You', 'Yes It Is', 'The Night Before', 'You Like Me Too Much', 'You've Got To Hide Your Love Away', 'If You've Got Trouble', 'Tell Me What You See', 'You're Gonna Lose That Girl', 'That Means A Lot'.

15 FEBRUARY
Lennon passes his driving test, though he remains at best an erratic driver, prone to dangerous lapses of concentration.
'Eight Days A Week' is pulled from the UK 'Beatles For Sale' album as a US single. It's another No. 1, of course.

22 FEBRUARY
The Beatles leave Britain for the Bahamas, where they are to film many of the location scenes for their second film, provisionally entitled *Eight Arms To Hold You*. Lennon is intrigued by the calm strength and mental agility of the group's co-star, Eleanor Bron. Meanwhile, the group settle into a steady routine of smoking pot whenever the cameras are turned off.

10/11 MARCH
The Beatles fly back from Nassau to London at the end of their first period of filming.

14 MARCH
Location filming for their next movie continues, this time in Austria.

18 MARCH
Hayling Supermarkets Ltd opens a store in Hayling Island, Hampshire – run by John's schoolfriend Pete Shotton, and financed with Lennon cash.

20 MARCH
The second set of film shoots is completed, leaving The Beatles free to return to Britain for the remaining footage to be taken.

22 MARCH
Capitol continue their regular pattern of Beatles releases with 'The Early Beatles', an 11-track selection from the 'Please Please Me' LP. The sixth US album to feature virtually the same tracks, it rises no higher than No. 43.

24 MARCH
Twickenham Film Studios is the latest location for work on *Eight Arms To Hold You*. They are based there through the end of the month, and again through most of April.

LATE MARCH
John and Cynthia are introduced to LSD by The Beatles' dentist, who slips impregnated sugar cubes into their after-dinner coffee. As their horizons expand and twist, they make their way circuitously to the Pickwick Club, where they mistake a small red light for a raging inferno. They survive this panic, and eventually find themselves at George's home, where John draws cartoons of The Beatles as a hydra, each head spouting the words 'We all agree with you'. Lennon's imagination never recovers from the extra dimension unveiled by this first psychedelic experience.

28 MARCH
Farewell to *Thank Your Lucky Stars*, as The Beatles grace its studios for the last time.

30 MARCH
The group return to Abbey Road and to 'That Means A Lot', one of the failures from their February sessions. Once again, the song is rejected.

Studio recording:
'That Means A Lot'.

1 APRIL
John and his father Freddie Lennon meet for the first time since the mid-Forties, when Freddie arrives on the Kenwood doorstep unannounced. Suspicious of his father's motives, John is unresponsive, bordering on hostile, during the encounter: "Where have you been for the last 20 years?" is his opening gambit.

He discovers that his father has been working as a dishwasher in a Hampton Court hotel. "His main object was to rip off some cash from John," says Cynthia. Freddie stays at Kenwood for three days, before Lennon throws him out.

6 APRIL
'Beatles For Sale' is the group's latest UK EP release.

9 APRIL
Lennon's 'Ticket To Ride' is released as the group's tenth UK single.

10 APRIL
As usual, The Beatles shoot a mimed performance of their new single for broadcast later on *Top Of The Pops*.

11 APRIL
The Beatles top the bill for the second year running at the *NME* Pollwinners Concert, held once again at the Empire Pool, Wembley. They subsequently appear live on *The Eamonn Andrews Show* on ITV.

American TV host Ed Sullivan with John, Ringo and Paul.

40

13 APRIL
On the surface, Lennon's 'Help!' – recorded today at Abbey Road – is another piece of superior craftsmanship, concocted when the title of The Beatles movie is changed from *Eight Arms To Hold You* to *Help!*. But the movie theme song disguises a set of self-revelatory lyrics that belie Lennon's brash, confident public image.

14 APRIL
Lennon and Harrison are interviewed live on *Ready, Steady, Go!*.

19 APRIL
'Ticket To Ride' appears as a US single, and spends just one week at No. 1.
   The Beatles win two Grammy Awards, from the American recording industry organisation, NARAS. Their prizes come for Best Group Performance, for 'A Hard Day's Night', and Best New Artists.

30 APRIL
The lengthy period of filming for *Help!* at Twickenham Film Studios is completed.

3 MAY
Location shooting for the movie resumes for several days, on Salisbury Plain.

9 MAY
The day passes in a whirl of London location filming. That evening, together with the other Beatles, Lennon attends Bob Dylan's acoustic concert at the Royal Albert Hall in London. Afterwards, the group and Dylan socialise cagily, each wary of the other's reputation.

10 MAY
For the last time with The Beatles, Lennon devotes himself to recording rock'n'roll covers. Despite production lapses, 'Dizzy Miss Lizzy' and 'Bad Boy' – both Larry Williams songs – bear rasping, superb Lennon vocals.
Studio recordings:
'Dizzy Miss Lizzy', 'Bad Boy'.

10/11 MAY
The 'Buckingham Palace' sequence for *Help!* is filmed at Cliveden.

18 MAY
The final day of filming and overdubbing on the *Help!* movie.

21 MAY
John and Cynthia fly to Cannes for the annual film festival.

25 MAY
John is interviewed in Cannes for US TV's *The Merv Griffin Show*. The Lennons return home later this afternoon.

26 MAY
The end of an era: The Beatles tape their final BBC radio session, broadcast two weeks later under the title *The Beatles Invite You To Take A Ticket To Ride*.
BBC recordings:
'Ticket To Ride', 'Everybody's Trying To Be My Baby', 'I'm A Loser', 'The Night Before', 'Honey Don't', 'Dizzy Miss Lizzy', 'She's A Woman', 'Ticket To Ride'.

4 JUNE
'Beatles For Sale (No. 2)' is released as a UK EP.

12 JUNE
It is announced in the morning papers that The Beatles are to be invested as Members of the British Empire (MBEs), for their "services to exports". Several war heroes return their medals in disgust.

14 JUNE
In a single recording session, Paul McCartney seizes the reins of the group's career from Lennon – who is absent as his partner tapes the timeless ballad 'Yesterday'.
Studio recordings:
'I've Just Seen A Face', 'I'm Down', 'Yesterday'.
   'Beatles VI' is the latest LP concocted for the American market, unveiling Lennon's romp through Larry Williams' 'Bad Boy' for the first time. Fans send it to No. 1, as usual.

> **"I'm selfish about what I write, or big-headed about it. Once I've done it, I like to keep it. But I always write it straight off. I might add things when I go over it, before it's published, but I seldom take anything out, so it's spontaneous".**

15 JUNE
Lennon's response to McCartney's mighty triple-play of the previous night is a song he subsequently regards as his weakest composition ever.

Studio recording:
'It's Only Love'.

16 JUNE
During two BBC Radio interviews, John takes the opportunity to plug his forthcoming book and recite his poems, 'The National Health Cow' and 'The Fat Budgie'.

John Lennon: "I'm selfish about what I write, or big-headed about it. Once I've done it, I like to keep it. But I always write it straight off. I might add things when I go over it, before it's published, but I seldom take anything out, so it's spontaneous."

17 JUNE
The final day of recording for the 'Help!' album.

Studio recordings:
'Act Naturally', 'Wait'.

18 JUNE
More advance promotional work for John's *A Spaniard In The Works* book, this time on BBC TV's *Tonight* show. Besides being interviewed once again by Kenneth Allsop, Lennon reads 'The Wumberlog' and 'We Must Not Forget The General Erection'.

20 JUNE
The Beatles fly from London to Paris to open their last full-scale European tour, with two shows at the Palais des Sports. Throughout the tour, concert venues are often less than half full – even in countries where The Beatles have never performed before.

22 JUNE
Two more shows, this time at the Winter Palace in Lyons.

24 JUNE
The group's first concert in Italy, at the Milan Velodrome.

Back in Britain, Lennon's second volume of poems, stories and drawings, *A Spaniard In The Works*, is published by Jonathan Cape. "I wrote it with a bottle of Johnnie Walker," he says many years later. The book is heavy with political cynicism and sarcasm, throws a couple of veiled verbal assaults in the direction of his errant father, and otherwise concentrates on nonsense at the expense of intelligibility. Significantly, though Lennon is offered a lucrative deal to write a third book for Cape, he abandons the attempt just before the proposed delivery date of his manuscript. In the future, his lyrical adventurism is concentrated upon his songs.

25 JUNE
Two shows at the Genoa Sports Palace. The first show has barely 20% of its seats filled.

27/28 JUNE
Four shows at the Adriano Theatre in Rome.

30 JUNE
Back to France, for a show at the Palais des Fêtes in Nice.

1 JULY
US publication date for *A Spaniard In The Works*.

2 JULY
The group's first show in Spain, at the Plaza de Toros de Madrid.

3 JULY
A farewell to arms after the last show of the tour, at the Plaza de Toros Monumental in Barcelona.

4 JULY
The Beatles return to London.

5 JULY
P.J. Proby releases Lennon/McCartney's 'That Means A Lot' for the first time.

13 JULY
Lennon and McCartney are presented with five Ivor Novello Awards in a London ceremony – except that Lennon neglects to turn up.

19 JULY
Lennon's 'Help!' becomes a US single, and a No. 1 for three weeks.

23 JULY
The title song from the *Help!* movie is issued as a UK single.

29 JULY
The *Help!* movie is premièred in London, with The Beatles – and John's Aunt Mimi – in attendance. Lennon later describes the film as "bullshit", and complains that "we were bit-players in our own movie".

1 AUGUST
Another performance on ITV's *Blackpool Night Out*, which includes a one-off impromptu version of 'I Do Like To Be Beside The Seaside'.

3 AUGUST
John takes his Aunt Mimi househunting in Bournemouth and Poole, eventually finding her a home overlooking Poole Harbour.

6 AUGUST
The patchy 'Help!' album is released in Britain.

13 AUGUST
Following the example of *A Hard Day's Night*, Capitol issue a soundtrack album from *Help!* which is divided between Beatles tracks and incidental music by the George Martin Orchestra. Despite the lack of authentic Beatles material, it spends more than two months at the top of the chart.

The group fly from London to New York to launch another US tour.

14 AUGUST
They tape a live set for *The Ed Sullivan Show*. Paul McCartney performs 'Yesterday', after which Lennon quips laconically: "Thank you, Paul. That was just like him."

15 AUGUST
The American tour begins with the biggest concert of their career, in front of nearly 56,000 fans at Shea Stadium in New York – the largest crowd ever assembled for a pop gig up to this date, and the highest-grossing show in history.

The entire proceedings, including some backstage footage, are taped for a TV movie, co-produced by Ed Sullivan's organisation and Brian Epstein and The Beatles' Subafilms Ltd.

During their stay in New York, Bob Dylan once again visits The Beatles; he and Lennon gradually build up a tentative rapport.

17 AUGUST
Two shows at Maple Leaf Gardens, Toronto, as The Beatles return to Canada.

18 AUGUST
Atlanta Stadium hosts The Beatles.

19 AUGUST
Two tumultuous shows at the Sam Houston Coliseum in Houston.

20 AUGUST
Two more shows, this time at White Sox Park in Chicago.

21 AUGUST
The Twin Cities Stadium in Minneapolis stages its evening of Beatles entertainment.

22 AUGUST
On to the Memorial Coliseum in Portland. En route, an engine on The Beatles' plane briefly catches fire; Lennon writes his obituary, and stashes it in a roll of film, as a 'momento' for posterity.

23 AUGUST
The group fly to Los Angeles for several days' rest at a Bel Air mansion. They receive visits from musicians like Bob Dylan and The Byrds – who take the opportunity to share drugs with The Beatles, and turn them on to the music of Ravi Shankar and John Coltrane.

In the midst of the madness, Lennon finds the time to write home to Cynthia: "I spend hours in dressing rooms and things thinking about the times I've wasted not being with Julian – and playing with him – you know I keep thinking of those stupid bastard times when I keep reading bloody newspapers and other shit whilst he's in the room with us and I've decided it's ALL WRONG! He doesn't see enough of me as it is and I really want him to know and love me, and miss me like I seem to be missing both of you so much.

"I'll go now 'cause I'm bringing myself down thinking what a thoughtless bastard I seem to be – I really feel like crying – it's so stupid – and I'm choking up now as I'm writing – I don't know what's the matter with me. I'm having lots of laughs, but in between the laughs there is such a drop. I love you very much..."

27 AUGUST
The much-hyped meeting between Elvis Presley and The Beatles takes place at Presley's Beverly Hills home. Lennon takes the opportunity to berate the King for the poor quality of his musical output since his return from the US Army; Presley subsequently campaigns secretly against The Beatles' pernicious influence over American youth.

During the same day, The Beatles hang out with The Byrds; that night, at an exclusive party in the Hollywood Hills, Lennon and Harrison take LSD for the second time, joined by members of The Byrds and budding actor Peter Fonda. Lennon is harassed by Fonda, who leans towards his ear and repeatedly whispers: "I know what it's like to be dead". The incident, fuelled by Fonda's

experiences during a major operation, subsequently inspires Lennon to write 'She Said She Said'.

Roger McGuinn (Byrds): "He kept telling John about his scar and how he'd been dead for a while. He had some sort of operation and had technically died and come back to life. We were all on acid and John couldn't take it in. It was morbid and bizarre."

28 AUGUST
Balboa Stadium in San Diego hosts The Beatles. After the show, several members of Presley's entourage visit the group, and discover that folksinger Joan Baez has joined their party, apparently infatuated by John.

29-30 AUGUST
Two shows at the Hollywood Bowl are once again taped for potential record release. In 1977, an album eventually appears selecting the best performances from the '64 and '65 Bowl concerts.

31 AUGUST
The tour ends at the Cow Palace in San Francisco.

SEPTEMBER
Given a month off from Beatles commitments, Lennon mooches around Kenwood, aware that life must have more to offer than this. He's depressed by the knowledge that McCartney is leading an active life on the London social scene, mingling with theatricals and artists while Lennon watches TV and waits for inspiration to strike.

10 SEPTEMBER
The only record with a 'produced by John Lennon and Paul McCartney' credit is released: The Silkie's version of John's 'You've Got To Hide Your Love Away'.

13 SEPTEMBER
McCartney's 'Yesterday' is released as a US single, and is listed on most charts as a solo record by Paul – prompting rumours that the group may split. No. 1? Of course.

25 SEPTEMBER
Fame leads The Beatles into a novel form of immortality, when their likenesses star in a US cartoon series simply entitled *The Beatles*. Actor Paul Frees doubles up as the voices of John and George.

8 OCTOBER
John and Paul release a single entitled 'People Say'. But it's not, as the public are obviously supposed to believe, *that* John and Paul.

11 OCTOBER
After a fairly quiet year, Capitol indulge themselves with another bout of Beatles repackaging, as they release six singles simultaneously: 'Twist And Shout', 'Love Me Do', 'Please Please Me', 'Do You Want To Know A Secret', 'Roll Over Beethoven' and 'Boys' (which crawls to No. 102).

12-13 OCTOBER
His creativity finally sparked by his drug experiences in America, Lennon brings the enigmatic 'Norwegian Wood' to the first 'Rubber Soul' session – though this startling version of the song remains unissued. Beneath the oblique lyrical imagery lies a bare confession of an extra-marital affair.

Studio recordings:
'Run For Your Life', 'Norwegian Wood', 'Drive My Car'.

16 OCTOBER
Lennon's 'Day Tripper', a metallic R&B song, is recorded with the memorable line, "She's a prick teaser" (or "big teaser", if you believe the official lyric sheet). "It was about a weekend hippie," he explains years later.

Studio recordings:
'Day Tripper', 'If I Needed Someone'.

18 OCTOBER
'In My Life' enters The Beatles' repertoire, as a nostalgic, bittersweet remembrance of Lennon's Liverpool life. By the time it is recorded, Lennon has excised the original street-by-street lyrical guide to the area in which he was raised, in favour of a

more general, but infinitely more moving, paean to friendship and the ever-present threat of loss.

Studio recordings:
'If I Needed Someone', 'In My Life'.

20, 21, 22, 24, 29 OCTOBER
'Norwegian Wood' is reworked during these Abbey Road sessions, while Lennon once again delves beneath the surface of the mainstream pop lyric to produce the confessional 'Nowhere Man' – its dense three-part vocal harmonies, like so much on 'Rubber Soul', proof of the impact that The Byrds' first album had made on The Beatles. Lyrically, the song hints at the emptiness of Lennon's life in Kenwood.

Studio recordings:
'We Can Work It Out', 'Norwegian Wood', 'Nowhere Man', 'In My Life', 'I'm Looking Through You'.

26 OCTOBER
The group interrupt the 'Rubber Soul' sessions to receive their MBE awards from the Queen at Buckingham Palace. Lennon smokes pot in the Palace toilets.

John Lennon: "All we did when we were waiting in the Palace was giggle. We collapsed, the whole thing was so funny. We knew in our hearts that the Queen was just some woman, yet we went through with it."

1/2 NOVEMBER
The Beatles take part in the filming of a Granada TV special, *The Music Of Lennon And McCartney*. Besides their own mimed performances of their new single, the show includes renditions of John and Paul's songs by a variety of other artists.

3, 4, 6, 8 NOVEMBER
Work continues on 'Rubber Soul', with Lennon's contribution restricted to joint lead guitar work on the rambling, unissued blues instrumental, '12-Bar Original'.

Studio recordings:
'Michelle', 'What Goes On', '12-Bar Original', 'I'm Looking Through You', 'Think For Yourself', 'The Beatles' Third Christmas Record'.

The Beatles pose with their MBEs.

11 DECEMBER
A second London gig, this time at the Finsbury Park Astoria.

12 DECEMBER
The last date of the final British tour by The Beatles takes place at the Capitol Cinema in Wales.

31 DECEMBER
John's father, Freddie Lennon, releases a single, on which he croons through two self-referential songs, 'That's My Life' and 'The Next Time You Feel Important'.

1966

JANUARY-MARCH
Having installed home recording equipment at Kenwood, Lennon begins to experiment with creating avant-garde pictures in sound, and equalling the mayhem of his prose writings with instruments. He also uses the facilities to cut one-man-band demos of his latest songs.

5 JANUARY
Subtly rewriting history, The Beatles re-record some of the dodgier musical performances from their summer 1965 Shea Stadium gig, for use on the soundtrack of the documentary film in production.

MID-JANUARY
Freddie Lennon turns up on his son's front doorstep, and is turned away. "It was only the second time in my life I'd seen him," John says a few weeks later. "I wasn't having *him* in the house."

FEBRUARY
Jonathan Cape are expecting the manuscript of Lennon's third book; instead, he returns the advance, and tells them to forget the deal.

21 FEBRUARY
Lennon's 'Nowhere Man' becomes the latest US single by The Beatles, but only reaches No. 3, although this is the song's first appearance in America.

10, 11 NOVEMBER
"The word is love," announces a new Lennon composition, introducing a theme that will survive in his work to the end. Equally typical, and far more impressive, is the ironic romantic reportage of his 'Girl' – perhaps the first pop song to tackle the subject of Catholic guilt about sex, and the Protestant work ethic. The song is introduced during the final day of recording on the 'Rubber Soul' album at Abbey Road.

Studio recordings:
'The Word', 'I'm Looking Through You', 'You Won't See Me', 'Girl', 'Wait'.

23 NOVEMBER
The Beatles film promo clips for their new single, plus belated promos for 'Help!', 'Ticket To Ride' and 'I Feel Fine', at Twickenham Film Studios. These clips subsequently reappear on TV stations around the world. It's a deliberate ploy to lessen the need for The Beatles to perform live in far-flung corners of the globe.

30 NOVEMBER
DJ Brian Matthew interviews Lennon about the group's latest recordings, for broadcast by the BBC overseas.

DECEMBER
An otherwise unpublished Lennon short story, 'The Toy Boy', is published in the American magazine *McCall's*. The piece, the sole refugee from John's attempt to concoct a third book, concludes with a sly self-reference: "He was an artiste, so you see, he didn't like to chime for free!"

3 DECEMBER
At Lennon's insistence, The Beatles' new UK single, 'Day Tripper'/'We Can Work It Out', is promoted as a double A-side release.
 The same day sees the release of 'Rubber Soul', an album which marks a definite artistic progression beyond The Beatles' earlier work.
 Finally, this day also sees the start of the final UK Beatles tour, at the Glasgow Odeon.

4 DECEMBER
On to Newcastle City Hall.

5 DECEMBER
For the final time, The Beatles perform live in Liverpool, at the Empire Theatre.

6 DECEMBER
'The Beatles' Million Sellers' is released as their latest UK EP.
 In the States, the 'Day Tripper'/'We Can Work It Out' single is released, while the US 'Rubber Soul' also appears – taking 10 tracks from the UK edition, alongside two leftovers from the British 'Help!' LP. Both releases top the American charts.

7 DECEMBER
The group perform at the Manchester ABC.

8 DECEMBER
Sheffield Gaumont is the next stop on the tour.

9 DECEMBER
South to the Birmingham Odeon.

10 DECEMBER
Hammersmith Odeon is the next venue.

MARCH

Lennon writes and records rough demos of a song provisionally entitled 'He Said He Said', and based around the acid-inspired comments of Peter Fonda during a Hollywood party eight months earlier.

4 MARCH

'Yesterday' is picked as the title track of The Beatles' new UK EP.

An interview with Lennon by Maureen Cleave is published in the London newspaper, the *Evening Standard*. During the encounter at his Weybridge, stockbroker-belt home, Lennon comments: "Christianity will go. It will vanish and shrink. I needn't argue about that; I'm right and I will be proved right. We're more popular than Jesus now. I don't know which will go first – rock'n'roll or Christianity. Jesus was all right, but his disciples were thick and ordinary. It's them twisting it that ruins it for me."

These comments spark intense controversy later in the year, but some of Lennon's other remarks hint at his future development: "Weybridge won't do at all. I'm just stopping at it, like a bus stop. I'll take my time; I'll get my real house when I know what I want. You see, there's something else I'm going to do, something I must do – only I don't know what it is. That's why I go round painting and taping and drawing and writing and that, because it may be one of them. All I know is, this isn't *it* for me."

25 MARCH

At a studio in West London, The Beatles tape interviews with Radio Caroline DJ Tom Lodge, and indulge in a customarily tame photo session for their official magazine, *The Beatles Book*. In between, they pose for the most remarkable photographs of their career, clad in butchers' overalls and clutching joints of raw meat and broken toy dolls. Photographer Robert Freeman, bent on surrealism, conducts the session; Lennon is his most willing disciple, keen to use the opportunity to shock The Beatles' audience out of their worshipful torpor. It is Lennon's

decision that one of the most brutal of the photos from this session should be used as the cover shot for their next US LP.

6 APRIL

The Beatles return to Abbey Road studios for their first session since November. They begin work on their next album with a song that marks every inch of their artistic development since they completed 'Rubber Soul' – Lennon's 'Tomorrow Never Knows'. Initially titled 'Mark 1' and then 'The Void', the song vividly conjures up the mental dislocation and spiritual quest unlocked by an LSD trip, with lyrics that borrow from *The Tibetan Book Of The Dead*.

At the session, Lennon tells producer George Martin that he wants to incorporate the sound of 4,000 monks chanting from a mountain-top. That problem is put on hold until the next day.

Studio recording:
'Tomorrow Never Knows'.

7, 8 APRIL

George Martin is unable to procure 4,000 monks for the afternoon's session, but does succeed in giving Lennon's voice an other-worldly air by feeding it through the Leslie speaker of a Hammond organ. 'Tomorrow Never Knows' gains its most disconcerting studio effects, however, from the use of tape loops made by The Beatles at Paul McCartney's suggestion. The finished recording is by far the most advanced piece of electronic and musical experimentation yet assembled by any pop performer.

Studio recording:
'Tomorrow Never Knows', 'Got To Get You Into My Life'.

11, 13, 14, 16 APRIL

Sessions continue at Abbey Road, among them the making of Lennon's remarkable 'Rain'. The song's weather imagery would be unexceptional were it not for the grim fatalism of Lennon's vocal, and the brilliant instrumental arrangement, hinged around what Ringo Starr believes to be his best-ever drumming on record. Lennon's voice is slowed down appreciably in the final mix, increasing the air of psychedelic

unreality; and the incorporation of a brief snatch of backwards tape is the crowning touch. Both Lennon and George Martin claim responsibility for this innovation, Lennon boasting that he'd taken a rough mix of the song home on April 14 while under the influence of cannabis, and inadvertently played it backwards.

Studio recordings:
'Got To Get You Into My Life', 'Love You To', 'Paperback Writer', 'Rain'.

17, 19 APRIL

Lennon and The Beatles cut a more lightweight tune, 'Doctor Robert', written in celebration of a medical man notorious for prescribing hallucinogenic drugs.

Studio recording:
'Doctor Robert'.

20-22 APRIL

'And Your Bird Can Sing', a joyously imprecise but gloriously raucous piece of pop-art, is Lennon's prime contribution to this batch of sessions.

Studio recordings:
'And Your Bird Can Sing', 'Taxman', 'Tomorrow Never Knows'.

25-29 APRIL

'And Your Bird Can Sing' is re-recorded during this week of sessions, but it pales alongside 'I'm Only Sleeping'. This Lennon composition is the drug-induced dream opposite to the nightmarish 'Tomorrow Never Knows'. John also helps Paul McCartney complete the lyrics to 'Eleanor Rigby', though he doesn't appear on the record.

Studio recordings:
'And Your Bird Can Sing', 'I'm Only Sleeping', 'Eleanor Rigby'.

1 MAY

For the last time, The Beatles appear on a British concert stage, as they top the bill at the *NME* Pollwinners' show at the Empire Pool, Wembley, for the third time. Lennon performs 'I Feel Fine', 'Nowhere Man' and 'Day Tripper', before taking a back seat on 'If I Needed Someone' and 'I'm Down'.

On the same day, ironically for those fans who attend the concert, the BBC chooses to première *The Beatles At Shea*

Stadium, a 50-minute documentary film of their concert in New York the previous August.

5, 6 MAY

Backwards guitar effects and trance-like vocals are added to 'I'm Only Sleeping'.

Studio recording:
'I'm Only Sleeping'.

9, 16, 18, 19 MAY

McCartney songs are the focus of these Beatle sessions.

Studio recordings:
'For No One', 'Taxman', 'Got To Get You Into My Life'.

19/20 MAY

Promo films for 'Paperback Writer' and 'Rain' are shot at Chiswick House in London and EMI House. Both clips neatly marry the traditions of previous Beatles TV appearances with hints of their new psychedelic demeanour.

26 MAY

Lennon takes full part in the session to record a vehicle for Ringo.

Studio recording:
'Yellow Submarine'.

27 MAY

John Lennon and George Harrison are present in a Royal Albert Hall box to watch Bob Dylan and The Hawks being catcalled and booed for performing a startlingly brilliant set of electric music rather than the acoustic folk with which Dylan was once linked.

Before the show, Dylan and Lennon share a taxi ride, filmed by D.A. Pennebaker, who is making a documentary of Dylan's tour. Both men are stoned; Dylan ends the sequence by vomiting over the floor of the cab.

30 MAY

Their new US single, 'Paperback Writer'/'Rain', announces that The Beatles have stepped beyond the conventions of the British beat scene – and breaks a long series of Lennon-composed A-sides. It reaches No. 1.

18 OCTOBER
How I Won The War is premièred in London. "I hate war," Lennon tells a reporter who asks why he took part in the film, "If there is another war I won't fight, and I'll try to tell all the youngsters not to fight either."

19, 20, 25 OCTOBER
Further recording sessions.

Studio recordings:
'Hello Goodbye', 'Fool On The Hill'.

2, 7 NOVEMBER
Work on the *Magical Mystery Tour* music is effectively completed.

10 NOVEMBER
Asserting his control over the group, Paul McCartney acts as director as The Beatles film three promo clips for their forthcoming single.

24 NOVEMBER
The Beatles release 'Hello Goodbye' as their next single, with Lennon's far more adventurous 'I Am The Walrus' relegated to the flipside. It reaches No. 1.
  Lennon begins work at Abbey Road on editing together tapes of sound effects for use in the forthcoming theatrical adaptation of sketches from his book, *In His Own Write*.

25 NOVEMBER
Lennon is interviewed about 'I Am The Walrus' by Kenny Everett on the BBC Radio 1 show, *Where It's At*. The song is then broadcast for the last time on the Beeb for several years, as senior producers soon decide it should be banned for its scandalous reference to 'knickers'.

27 NOVEMBER
Capitol release 'Hello Goodbye', and also the 'Magical Mystery Tour' album – which features the new songs from the TV special, alongside the group's other 1967 singles. Both records top their respective US charts.

28 NOVEMBER
The Beatles record a psychedelic seasonal song, after which Lennon prepares more sound effect tapes.

Studio recording:
'Christmas Time Is Here Again'.

DECEMBER
Victor Spinetti stages one performance of *Scene Three, Act One*, a one-act play he and Adrienne Kennedy have adapted from Lennon's first book, *In His Own Write*. The play is later renamed after the book.

5 DECEMBER
Lennon and Harrison attend a launch party for a new Beatles enterprise, the Apple Boutique.

8 DECEMBER
Parlophone release a double-EP set of songs from *Magical Mystery Tour*: Lennon's sole composition is 'I Am The Walrus', already available on a single.

11 DECEMBER
Lennon okays the first signing to The Beatles' Apple Music publishing company, and renames them Grapefruit after Yoko's book of the same title. Around this time, he and McCartney produce their début single, 'Dear Delilah', adding some of the 1965-era Beatles panache to the project.

21 DECEMBER
At a party at London's Royal Lancaster Hotel to celebrate the imminent broadcast of *Magical Mystery Tour*, Lennon attends dressed as a 50s Teddy Boy. He takes a more than friendly interest in fellow guest Pattie Harrison, until reprimanded by singer Lulu and reminded that his own wife is his escort for the evening.

26 DECEMBER
Magical Mystery Tour is premièred on BBC2, and receives a savage reception from the critics – and from a large section of the public, who are expecting more traditional Bank Holiday fare.

29 DECEMBER
John begins a week's vacation in Morocco, while McCartney tries to salvage The Beatles' media reputation.

1968

JANUARY
Lennon's estranged father, Freddie Lennon, phones his son to inform him that he is planning to marry a 19-year-old student, Pauline Jones. Lennon finds Pauline a job as his secretary, until the family tension becomes too much.

12 JANUARY
The Beatles' new company, Apple Corps Ltd., is registered in London, as is sister business Apple Films Ltd. For its initial year, Apple is very much Paul McCartney's brainchild; John Lennon approves the principle, but would rather someone else did the work.

22 JANUARY
Apple Corps opens for business at 95 Wigmore Street, London W1.

25 JANUARY
After originally swearing to have as little as possible to do with the making of the *Yellow Submarine* movie, The Beatles are filmed in London for the closing sequence of the film.

27 JANUARY
DJ Kenny Everett interviews Lennon at home for BBC Radio 1.

3, 4, 6, 8 FEBRUARY
The Beatles tape a new single, and also record a new Lennon song, 'Across The Universe'. Its lyrics reflect the liberation of poetic inspiration, but The Beatles fail to catch that spirit in their recording of the song – despite pulling in two fans from the Abbey Road car park to sing backing vocals.

Studio recording:
'Lady Madonna', 'Across The Universe', 'The Inner Light'.

11 FEBRUARY
Attending Abbey Road to be filmed for a 'Lady Madonna' promo clip, The Beatles elect to record Lennon's anarchic rocker, 'Hey Bulldog'. Also in the studio for the first time at a Beatles session is Yoko Ono, who diplomatically asks Lennon while the group always use such simplistic rhythms in their songs.

Studio recording:
'Hey Bulldog'.

15 FEBRUARY
The Lennons and Harrisons leave London for India, and the Maharishi's camp at Rishikesh. The other Beatles join them four days later. For the next two months, the group attempts to adjust itself to a regime of meditation and contemplation, enlivened by occasional jam sessions with fellow guests like Donovan and Beach Boys' vocalist Mike Love.
  Lennon, McCartney and Harrison all compose new material during this transcendental experience. Lennon's songs range in mood from the beneficent idealism of 'The Happy Rishikesh Song' and 'Child Of Nature', to the naked self-doubt, verging on self-loathing, of 'Yer Blues' and 'I'm So Tired'. Other new compositions, like 'Julia' and 'Look At Me', reflect the influence of Donovan, who teaches Lennon an acoustic picking style during the weeks of meditation.

29 FEBRUARY
Yoko Ono guests at a concert by avant-garde jazzman Ornette Coleman at the Royal Albert Hall. This is merely the latest in

53

a long sequence of Ono concert appearances stretching back to New York in 1961, when she performed 'Voice Piece For Soprano' at the Village Gate. Later that year, she performed *A Grapefruit In The World Of Park*, "a piece for strawberries and violin", at Carnegie Recital Hall. Since then, music has been a regular feature of her performance art.

Both the concert and the rehearsals are taped; an extract from Yoko's 'Aos', from the afternoon rehearsal, is included two years later on the 'Yoko Ono Plastic Ono Band' LP.

MARCH

Yoko Ono and her husband Tony Cox separate. From her home in Hanover Square, London W1, she writes regularly to Lennon in India. Her correspondence becomes little less than a fusillade when Lennon returns to Britain. Among the items she sends him are the manuscripts of 'Sky Event For John Lennon/spring 1968' and 'Sky Event II': both suggest that two performers can be as one, even if they're separated by thousands of miles. Another Ono prose piece from this period is 'John Lennon As A Young Cloud'. Lennon can't help but be flattered.

9 MARCH

'Sgt. Pepper' wins four Grammy Awards in New York, among them the prizes for the year's best album, and the best album cover.

15 MARCH

'Lady Madonna' becomes the latest Beatles single. For the first time, neither side of the record bears any recognisable input from Lennon.

In Rishikesh, The Beatles serenade Beach Boys' vocalist Mike Love with a specially composed ditty, 'Happy Birthday Michael Love', which segues into another half-baked tune called 'Spiritual Regeneration'. The acoustic performances are preserved on tape. By now, the mood at the Maharishi's is becoming restless; Ringo Starr is missing his home cooking, and Lennon is starting to find that

the clearing of the mind induced by meditation is leading as often to cynicism as to inner peace.

18 MARCH

America greets 'Lady Madonna' in mixed fashion, as the single only makes No. 4.

MID-APRIL

Lennon's misgivings about the meditation experience explode into outright opposition, after his friend 'Magic' Alex Mardas suggests that the Maharishi has been showing a less than spiritual interest in actress Mia Farrow. McCartney and Starr have already fled for Britain; now Lennon and Harrison spike each other into a state of deep suspicion, whereupon Lennon – "I was always the leader when dirty work needed doing," he notes sardonically later – is deputed to confront the Maharishi. "We're going home," he says bluntly, and when the guru asks why, Lennon snaps: "If you're so fucking cosmic, you should know."

As ever, when he's let down by a father figure, Lennon reacts with violence: his disgust is channelled into an obscene rant called 'Maharishi', which subsequently assumes milder form as 'Sexy Sadie'.

20 APRIL

Apple begin running ads in the music press soliciting demo tapes, poetry manuscripts, film scripts and other suggestions of a vaguely artistic nature. This attempt to involve the public in mass creativity ends in chaos, as the Apple offices are swamped with unopened packages.

LATE APRIL

The Lennons and Harrisons return home from India. On the flight, John informs Cynthia that he has been unfaithful to her with dozens of women – groupies, actresses, protest singers and journalists – since their marriage. Cynthia is stunned, but forces herself to regard the episode as a rebirth, rather than a conclusion. However, she goes on holiday to Greece soon after the couple arrive home.

9 MAY

John, Ringo, Derek Taylor, 'Magic' Alex Mardas and The Beatles' old Liverpool friend, Ivan Vaughan, meet at Apple to plan the founding of an idealistic school for the children of The Beatles and their staff.

11 MAY

Lennon and McCartney fly to New York to announce the formation and utopian purpose of Apple Corps.

14 MAY

Lennon and McCartney appear on NBC-TV's *The Tonight Show*, with guest-host Joe Garagiola floundering as the pair attempt to explain the ideals behind the formation of Apple. Lennon also manages a blast at America's involvement in Vietnam: "It's insanity". He also tells America that the solution to political injustice is "to change the establishment".

16 MAY

Lennon and McCartney return to London.

19 MAY

During a business meeting at Apple, a psychedelically-influenced John Lennon announces to the rest of The Beatles that he is the Messiah. They greet the news calmly, and move on to other business.

20 MAY

While Cynthia Lennon is away on holiday, John Lennon invites Yoko Ono to his house. The couple indulge in some experimental music-making, extracts from which appear as the 'Two Virgins' album at the end of the year, before making love for the first time.

John Lennon: "I called her over. Cyn was away and I thought, 'Well, now's the time if I'm gonna get to know her any more'. She came to my house and I didn't know what to do, so we went upstairs to my studio and I played her all the tapes that I'd made, some comedy stuff and some electronic music. She was suitably impressed and said, 'Let's make one ourselves'. So we made 'Two Virgins'. It was midnight when we started, it

was dawn when we finished, and then we made love at dawn. It was very beautiful."

21 MAY

Cynthia Lennon returns from Greece one afternoon to discover John and Yoko sitting calmly in dressing-gowns in the kitchen of the Lennons' home. She realises that Yoko is wearing her gown. "Oh, hi," says Lennon distractedly. Cynthia flees in panic, aware that her marriage is over. As an ineffectual form of escape, she spends the night with Apple electronics head Alex Mardas. She returns a few days later to Kenwood, however, and life with the Lennons briefly continues as if nothing has happened.

25 MAY

The Beatles begin several days of recording at George Harrison's home, assembling shambolic but endearing acoustic demos of the material they've written during their stay in India. Even the fiery rhetoric of 'Revolution' assumes a wide-eyed, pot-fuelled innocence amidst a cloud of marijuana smoke.

28 MAY

After three days of hazy goodwill towards Beatles and mankind, Lennon veers back towards violence, as he records a vicious talkin' blues called 'The Maharishi Song' with Yoko in his home studio. Besides the giggling guru, Cynthia and the other Beatles wives feel the sting of Lennon's jagged sarcasm.

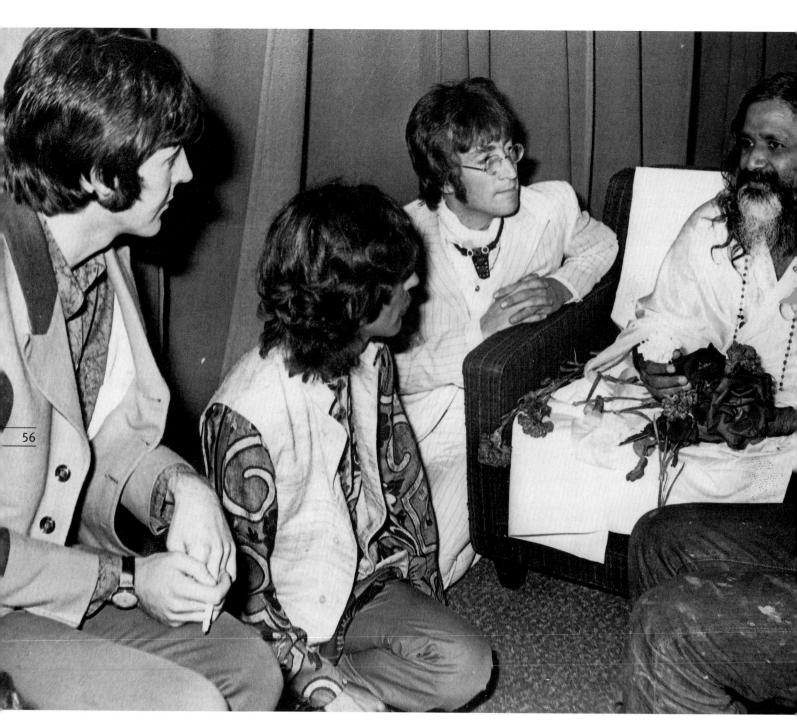

56

The Maharishi Mahesh Yogi with his
most famous converts.

"Come and join us," says writer John Hoyland in his 'Open Letter To John Lennon'. Lennon subsequently phones *Black Dwarf* editor Tariq Ali, who invites him to write a response.

4 NOVEMBER
Yoko Ono is admitted to Queen Charlotte's Hospital in London because of complications in her pregnancy.

7 NOVEMBER
Lennon draws a strip cartoon entitled 'A Short Essay On Macrobiotics' for the magazine *Harmony*.

8 NOVEMBER
Cynthia Lennon is granted a divorce *nisi* from John.

John and Yoko take out advertisements in the British pop papers to support The Peace Ship, a radio station attempting to bring relief to the ongoing Arab/Israeli conflict.

11 NOVEMBER
The delayed US release date of one of the most controversial albums in history – John Lennon and Yoko Ono's 'Unfinished Music No. 1 – Two Virgins'. The 29-minute collage of sound effects, dialogue, musical experimentation and semi-inspired lunacy passes almost unnoticed, as attention is focused on the album's cover, which features nude photographs of the couple.

The cover also includes a one-line note from Paul McCartney, which suggests he supports the project; but it subsequently emerges that he has been negotiating behind the scenes to persuade John not to release it.

EMI and Capitol both refuse to distribute the album. Eventually, it reaches US shops only when it is cloaked in a plain brown wrapper, and handled by the indie label Tetragrammaton. It doesn't chart for several months, as the indie's distribution takes time to swing into action, and peaks at No. 124.

John Lennon: "Originally, I was going to record Yoko, and I thought the best picture of her for an album would be her naked. So after that, when we got together, it just seemed natural for both of us to be naked. Of course, I've never seen me prick out on an album before."

Yoko Ono: "EMI wouldn't touch it."

MID-NOVEMBER
John and Yoko hire Nick Knowland's film crew to make *Rape*, a movie in which a young woman – unaware of the purpose of the pursuit – is chased around the streets of London in metaphoric enactment of the film's title. After the 'excitement' of the chase, where the hand-held cameras come close to inducing audience sea-sickness, the final 40 minutes of the film take place in a darkened room, in which the woman is attempting to take refuge from the insidious assault of the camera. From Yoko's 1968 notes on *Film Script No. 5: Rape (or Chase)*: "A cameraman will chase a girl on a street with a camera persistently until he corners her in an alley and, if possible, until she is in a falling position. The cameraman will be taking a risk of offending the girl as the girl is somebody he picks up arbitrarily on the street. May chase boys and men as well."

From Yoko's programme notes when the film is premièred: "Violence is a sad wind that, if channelled carefully, could bring seeds, chairs and all things pleasant to us... We go on eating and feeding frustration every day, lick lollipops and stay being peeping-toms dreaming of becoming Jack-The-Ripper.

"This film was shot by our cameraman, Nick, while we were in a hospital. Nick is a gentleman, who prefers eating clouds and floating pies to shooting *Rape*. Nevertheless it was shot. And as John says: 'A is for parrot, which we can plainly see'."

21 NOVEMBER
After more than two weeks of hospital treatment, Yoko Ono suffers a miscarriage. Their 24-week-old foetus is named John Ono Lennon II, and buried secretly. The baby's fading heartbeats were recorded by John, and subsequently released on the 'Life With The Lions' album. During Yoko's hospital stay, the couple also chant extracts from their own news clippings ('No Bed For Beatle John') and mess about with a radio ('Radio Play').

22 NOVEMBER
'The Beatles' distracts the outside world from 'Two Virgins'. This two-LP, 30-track masterpiece reveals a group who are able to pastiche any musical style from hard rock to crooning, via reggae, soul, jazz and avant-garde. It also highlights the growing musical rifts between the individual band members, although for the moment these are restrained by the need to keep The Beatles intact as a unit. The result is a record made under extreme tension, which fuels its artistic innovation and brilliance. The plain white packaging, in direct contrast to the lavish opulence of 'Sgt. Pepper', proves to be just as influential as the music.

25 NOVEMBER
Yoko Ono is discharged from Queen Charlotte's Hospital.

'The Beatles' is released in America, where it tops the charts into March.

28 NOVEMBER
At Marylebone Magistrates Court in London, Lennon pleads guilty to a charge of possessing cannabis resin, and is fined £150, plus 20 guineas costs. The charges of obstruction against John and Yoko are dropped. His drugs conviction is to have unforeseen repercussions for the next eight years, as it jeopardises his ability to enter the USA.

29 NOVEMBER
'Two Virgins' reaches British stores, but only under wraps – and thanks to the intervention of Track Records, who handle the distribution in a one-off deal.

On the same day, Lennon fills in a cheap 1969 diary with parody entries, and donates the result to the art magazine *Aspen*.

EARLY DECEMBER
His baby son dead, his future entry to the States jeopardised by his drugs conviction, his relations with the rest of The Beatles under severe strain, Lennon once again takes refuge in the twin consolations of art and heroin. "We took heroin because we were artists," explains Yoko helpfully in later years.

Around this time, in the wintry surroundings of Kenwood, Lennon composes a self-pitying ballad, 'Everybody Had A Hard Year', the self-explanatory 'A Case Of The Blues' and – in a rare burst of optimism – a love song for Yoko, 'Don't Let Me Down'. But all these songs pale alongside the first draft of 'Oh My Love', written for Yoko to sing: far from its ultimate fate as a romantic idyll, this is a haunting song of love and regret for the couple's lost child.

The BBC film John in his garden, picking desultorily at his acoustic guitar and singing his 'Hard Year' blues.

10 DECEMBER
Rehearsals are held for The Rolling Stones' TV special, in which John and Yoko have agreed to take part.

11 DECEMBER
Lennon and Ono perform in *The Rolling Stones Rock'n'Roll Circus*, filmed today but still unreleased at the time of writing – although Polygram Video were reportedly editing the raw tapes in early 1995. The Lennons' contribution comprises a wild eight-minute version of 'Yer Blues', which segues into an instrumental jam. They are backed by Keith Richard, Eric Clapton and Mitch Mitchell, plus a guest violinist for the latter sections of the jam.

Between takes, Lennon jams on Sun Records rockabilly classics with Taj Mahal's guitarist Jesse Ed Davis – who soon becomes a regular part of The Beatles' extended musical family, playing on many solo recordings by group members in the Seventies.

That evening, John and Yoko are interviewed by DJ John Peel

on BBC Radio's *Night Ride* show, in which extracts from the 'Two Virgins' LP are broadcast.

18 DECEMBER
As an 'Alchemical Wedding' is staged by various underground art and politics groups at the Royal Albert Hall in London, John and Yoko crawl on stage — clad in a white bag. 'Bagism' is officially born, though Yoko has already been filmed earlier in 1968 walking the streets of the West End in a white sack, and has been performing 'Bag Piece' in her live shows since 1962.

The birth of the couple's political radicalism can also be traced to this event, when a spectator interrupts their 'appearance' by parading in front of the stage with a banner complaining that British government involvement in the dispute in Nigeria is leading to thousands of Biafrans dying of starvation. "Do you care, John Lennon, do you care?" cries the anonymous protestor. John mulls it over.

23 DECEMBER
John and Yoko play Father and Mother Christmas to a mixed group of staff, children and visiting Hell's Angels at Apple's Christmas Party.

1969

JANUARY
Lennon's 'very open letter' to the editors of *Black Dwarf* is published in the newspaper's first issue of 1969. "We set up Apple with the money we as workers earned," he wrote, "so that we could control what we did production-wise. I'll tell you what's wrong with the world: people – so do you want me to destroy them? Who fucked up Communism, Christianity, Capitalism, Buddhism etc.? Sick heads and nothing else." His piece concludes: "You smash it – and I'll build around it."

In Hartford, Connecticut, the University authorities ban the campus newspaper, after it includes the front and back cover illustrations of the 'Two Virgins' album. The furore is reported to the FBI, who open a file on John Lennon.

2 JANUARY
The Beatles assemble at Twickenham Film Studios to begin work on a nebulous movie project. At various stages over the next four weeks of tortured and tortuous sessions, they claim to be (a) recording a new album; (b) rehearsing for a live concert, to be filmed for TV; (c) filming a documentary about either or both of the above; (d) any combination of all of these.

The first day's session begins at an inordinate hour for the benefit of the film crew, and is staged in a vast studio many times the size of anything The Beatles have recorded in before. At Twickenham, cameras and microphones are running throughout the sessions, though nothing is being taped for record release.

Lennon brings two nearly complete songs to this session, 'Don't Let Me Down' and 'Everyone Had A Hard Year'. He also takes the opportunity to complain vigorously about the impersonality of the setting.

3 JANUARY
The group jam fitfully through a batch of rock'n'roll oldies, and unearth one of their own – 'The One After 909', which they recorded but didn't release in 1963. Lennon makes his boredom felt as The Beatles turn their attention to Harrison's 'All Things Must Pass'. He also toys with an early version of his 'Imagine' song, 'Gimme Some Truth'.

Police in Newark, New Jersey, USA, seize thousands of copies of John and Yoko's 'Two Virgins' LP, claiming that its open sale contravenes pornography laws.

6 JANUARY
The rehearsal sessions meander along, before the band break to discuss the direction of their project. Lennon remains silent throughout, leaving Yoko to make increasingly bizarre suggestions on his behalf. While Paul, George and Ringo debate the size of the audience they should perform to, Yoko reckons they should play only to members of the royal family, or perhaps be filmed performing in their homes, rather than in public. Disastrous renditions of 'Don't Let Me Down' and McCartney's 'Two Of Us' follow, Lennon still refusing to make any creative decisions.

7 JANUARY
During long arguments with Paul McCartney, George Harrison suggests that The Beatles should split up. Lennon says nothing. The group then attempt to rehearse McCartney's 'Maxwell's Silver Hammer', sabotaged by Lennon's indifference. When they move on to 'Across The Universe', he is apparently unable to recall the words to his own song.

8 JANUARY
Back at Twickenham, The Beatles bicker their way through another day. Lennon constantly maligns Harrison's songwriting, but shows little enthusiasm for contributing anything substantial of his own.

9 JANUARY
Another day, another rehearsal: The Beatles try and consolidate on the songs they've practised over the previous week, but Lennon's inability to remember the words or the arrangements hampers them. In the midst of the chaos, there's a beacon of light, as they improvise an original 12-bar blues called 'Suzy Parker'. That sets the standard for the rest of the day, during which they jam round non-existent songs, with lyrics made up of the names of friends, enemies and people in the news.

10 JANUARY
During a lunch break in today's rehearsals, Harrison confronts Lennon over his lack of involvement in the sessions. Lennon replies with a mixture of silence and contempt, whereupon Harrison announces he is leaving The Beatles, and walks out of the sessions. This seems to lighten Lennon's mood: when the remaining three Beatles resume work after lunch, John amuses himself by calling for the absent George to take solos.

12 JANUARY
All four Beatles gather at Ringo Starr's house to discuss their problems; the feud between Harrison and Lennon remains intractable.

13 JANUARY
When the day's rehearsals are scheduled to begin, just two Beatles attend, McCartney and Starr. Lennon makes a brief appearance late in the afternoon, almost as a gesture of contempt for the group. In his absence, Paul and Ringo discuss the difficulty of dealing with John when he has apparently appointed Yoko to speak and act on his behalf.

The 'Yellow Submarine' soundtrack album is released in the States, featuring one side of Beatles' material, and one of incidental music by the George Martin Orchestra. The LP provides the first airing of Lennon's superbly arch rocker, 'Hey Bulldog'. It reaches No. 2, behind 'The Beatles'.

14 JANUARY
Lennon turns up for this day's session, to complain that he's taken too many drugs the previous night, and hasn't been to bed. Eventually, he leads the three-man Beatles through a medley of two new songs-in-progress, 'Madman' and 'Watching Rainbows'.

15 JANUARY
Lennon and Harrison make their peace at a band meeting, and The Beatles agree to shift their sessions from Twickenham to Apple's own studio, and to begin recording rather than necessarily working towards a possible live show.

16 JANUARY
In the edition of *Disc And Music Echo* which goes on sale today, Lennon is quoted as saying that Apple is losing vast quantities of money, and that The Beatles are in danger of going bankrupt unless the situation is reversed. US pop manager Allen Klein reads the story with interest.

17 JANUARY
'Yellow Submarine' reaches British stores.

20 JANUARY
The Beatles arrive at Apple, but abandon plans to record when they discover that their studio equipment is faulty.

22 JANUARY
Regrouping at Apple's newly-enhanced studio in Savile Row, The Beatles run through a desultory morning rehearsal, before the introduction of keyboard player Billy Preston into the sessions imposes some long-overdue discipline into their work.

Studio recordings:
'Dig A Pony', 'I've Got A Feeling', 'Don't Let Me Down', 'Save The Last Dance For Me', plus assorted jams and off-cuts.

23 JANUARY
Lennon, McCartney, Ono and Preston indulge in a free-form jam between endless versions of 'Get Back'.

Studio recording:
'Get Back'.

24 JANUARY
A long day of rehearsals, jams and recordings, during which Lennon leads the group through an impromptu number called 'Dig It', exhumes a song called 'I Lost My Little Girl' from the 1950s Lennon/McCartney songbook, and attempts to persuade the other Beatles that Billy Preston should become a full-time member of the group. McCartney turns this suggestion down.

Studio recordings:
'Two Of Us', 'Teddy Boy', 'Maggie Mae', 'Dig It', 'Dig A Pony', 'I've Got A Feeling'.

25 JANUARY
One of the less productive days from the sessions filmed at Apple.

Studio recordings:
'Two Of Us', 'For You Blue', 'Let It Be'.

26 JANUARY
Several of the highlights of the *Let It Be* movie were taped during this day's work, including some of the group's more

coherent rock'n'roll numbers, and the extended jam on 'Dig It'.

Studio recording:
'Dig It', 'Let It Be', 'The Long And Winding Road', plus several rock'n'roll covers.

27 JANUARY
John interrupts the day's first performance to inform the rest of the group that Yoko's divorce from Anthony Cox has just been confirmed.

Studio recordings:
'Get Back', 'Oh! Darling', 'I've Got A Feeling'.

28 JANUARY
Lennon arrives late (as usual) for the day's session as he's been invited to a meeting with Allen Klein, who is keen to state his case for managing The Beatles' business empire. Despite his awareness of Klein's unscrupulous reputation, first-hand knowledge of which he's picked up from the manager's previous clients, The Rolling Stones, Lennon is impressed, and begins suggesting the idea to his fellow Beatles. Meanwhile, Paul McCartney is lobbying the group to enlist Lee Eastman, the father of Paul's girlfriend Linda, as their business adviser.

Back in the studio, before recording the songs listed below, The Beatles rehearse several numbers that will emerge later in the year, like 'Something', 'Old Brown Shoe' and 'I Want You (She's So Heavy)'.

Studio recordings:
'Dig A Pony', 'Get Back', 'Don't Let Me Down', 'I've Got A Feeling', 'The One After 909'.

29 JANUARY
Having agreed that they will perform 'live' on the Apple roof the next day, The Beatles devote themselves to light-hearted rehearsals.

Studio recordings:
'The One After 909' plus various covers.

30 JANUARY
For the final time, The Beatles perform in public, to an audience of wives, aides, cameramen and eventually a handful of Metropolitan

Policemen. On the roof of their Apple HQ, they blast through 40 minutes of good-humoured, and surprisingly coherent, live performances, before the police arrive in response to complaints from local businessmen that they are disrupting the normal business activity of the Savile Row area. "I hope we passed the audition," Lennon announces at the end of their set.

Studio recordings:
'Get Back', 'Don't Let Me Down', 'I've Got A Feeling', 'The One After 909', 'Dig A Pony'.

31 JANUARY
Safely indoors at Apple, the group run studiously through three more numbers which have been arranged to their satisfaction, performing multiple takes for the cameras until they're satisfied with the results. After take 27B of 'Let It Be', their movie project is put on hold while the group try to forget it ever happened. Various attempts are made over the next year to find a satisfactory structure for the hours of films

and tapes made this month, but it is more than a year before the group are able to agree on a solution – and even then Paul McCartney, whose enthusiasm has been vital in keeping the group alive through its recent turmoil, is apparently not consulted. We're left with the irony that the best-documented month of The Beatles' career is also their least productive and most self-destructive.

Studio recordings:
'The Long And Winding Road', 'Let It Be', 'Two Of Us'.

FEBRUARY
Lennon writes the acrostic poem 'This Is My Story Both Humble And True', included alongside his erotic lithographs in his *Bag One* collection.

2 FEBRUARY
Yoko Ono's divorce from film-maker Anthony Cox is officially ratified. Yoko is granted custody of their daughter, Kyoko Cox.

3 FEBRUARY

Lennon having won the argument, for the moment, Allen Klein becomes The Beatles' business manager – or as the press release puts it, "The Beatles have asked Mr Klein to look into all their affairs, and he has agreed to do so".

4 FEBRUARY

Tit for tat: Lennon agrees to the appointment of Lee Eastman as the group's chief legal adviser. Conflict is inevitable.

22/23 FEBRUARY

With the movie project left in limbo, The Beatles tentatively start work on another record. They commence with 'I Want You (She's So Heavy)', a stark Lennon love song inspired lyrically by Yoko and musically by Mel Torme's 'Coming Home Baby'.

Studio recordings:
'I Want You (She's So Heavy)'.

MARCH

The art 'magazine' *Aspen* publishes its seventh issue, which comprises a number of different sections and objects packaged in a box. Section 8 is a book entitled 'The Lennon Diary 1969' (written on 29th November 1968); Section 11 is a flexi-disc, featuring John and Yoko's 'Radio Play' collage, 'No Bed For Beatle John', a spoken collection of press clippings, and 'Song For John', a medley of unaccompanied Yoko Ono songs.

The March issue of *Nova* magazine features an interview with the Lennons, during which Yoko utters the fateful phrase: "Woman is the nigger of the world".

2 MARCH

John and Yoko make their first concert appearance together, during an evening of avant-garde jazz and experimental music at Lady Mitchell Hall, Cambridge University. With the aid of jazz musicians John Tchikai and John Stevens, they perform one improvised piece, later titled 'Cambridge 1969', with Yoko ad-libbing vocally over John's thunderous guitar feedback.

12 MARCH

Paul McCartney and Linda Eastman are married; George and Pattie Harrison are busted for drugs. John and Yoko aren't present for either event. Instead, they are at Abbey Road, recording 'Peace Song'. This may or may not be the same as 'Rock Peace', an instrumental Plastic Ono Band single briefly scheduled for release later in 1969.

Studio recording:
'Peace Song'.

16 MARCH

John and Yoko have decided to get married, but not in Britain. Their first choice of venue is a cross-channel ferry, but they are denied permission to board the *Dragon* at Southampton Docks because of "inconsistencies in their passports". Instead, they fly to Paris, where they spend four days planning their next move.

20 MARCH

John Winston Lennon and Yoko Ono are married at the British Consulate on the territory of Gibraltar. Beatles aide Peter Brown is there to act as witness. Afterwards, the couple pose for the official photographs, taken by David Nutter – Lennon in a white suit, Ono in matching white minidress and hat.

The couple have flown by private jet from Paris to Gibraltar early in the morning, and landed on the Rock at 8.30am. They arrive at the British Consulate at 9.00am, where they are met by registrar Cecil Wheeler, who conducts the ceremony.

John Lennon: "We chose Gibraltar because it is quiet, British and friendly. We tried everywhere else first. I set out to get married on the car ferry and we would have arrived in France married. But they wouldn't do it. We were no more successful with cruise ships. We tried embassies. But three weeks' residence in Germany or two weeks' in France were required."

After the service, the newly-weds fly back to Paris, and their luxury suite at the Plaza Athenée Hotel.

John and Yoko backstage at London's
Lyceum Ballroom with, amongst others,
Eric Clapton, Keith Moon and George
Harrison, after The Plastic Ono Band's
Peace for Christmas concert.

1 JULY
During a Scottish holiday with
their children, Julian and Kyoko,
the Lennons are involved in a
serious car crash near Golspie
while John – at best, an
inexperienced driver – is at the
wheel. All four members of the
family are kept in hospital
overnight. Yoko is the most
seriously injured, suffering from
crushed vertebrae and
concussion. Lennon receives 17
stitches for a head wound.

3 JULY
The Lennons' injuries prevent
them from attending the official
launch of their first solo record,
'Give Peace A Chance', under the
name of the Plastic Ono Band.
Ringo Starr deputises, while a
multi-media console (seen on
the picture cover for the single)
is introduced at the Chelsea
Town Hall party as the Plastic
Ono Band. Guests are handed
clear plastic boxes, each
containing an acorn sitting in a
bed of cotton-wool. The acorn is
designed to be planted for

peace; the packaging is
destined for the trash. 'Give
Peace A Chance' is played over
the Town Hall PA for three hours
until the guests get the message
and go home.

4 JULY
The world is introduced to the
Plastic Ono Band, as 'Give Peace
A Chance'/'Remember Love' is
released in Britain.

6 JULY
The Lennons hire a private jet
to fly them home to London.
Meanwhile, their smashed car is
crushed into a metallic cube and
exhibited as a sculpture in the
grounds of Tittenhurst Park.

7 JULY
The US release date for 'Give
Peace A Chance', which again
suffers restricted airplay, and
stalls at No. 14.

9-11 JULY
After more than a week in which
the remaining Beatles have
worked without him, Lennon
returns to Abbey Road,

to help him coin a deliciously mean couplet: "The only thing you done was Yesterday/And since you gone you're just Another Day".

Also written at this time are 'Oh Yoko', building on a demo cut late the previous year; 'God Save Us', written under commission from journalists at the magazine *Oz*; and 'Call My Name', a mournful piano ballad that is subsequently rewritten as 'Aisumasen'.

1 JUNE
In a vain attempt to raise funds for the beleaguered underground journal *Oz*, Lennon records a benefit single entitled 'God Save Us'. After steering a hastily assembled band through the song with a guide vocal, he allows Apple Publishing writer Bill Elliott to sing the lead. With John and Yoko's avant-rock 'Do The Oz' as the flipside, the single is ready for release by 'Bill Elliott & the Elastic Oz Band'.

Studio recordings:
'God Save Us', 'Do The Oz'.

3 JUNE
John and Yoko jet to New York in search of Tony & Melinda Cox, though they spend their first afternoon shopping in Greenwich Village.

6 JUNE
In the afternoon, the Lennons appear on Howard Smith's talk show on WPLJ radio. That night, John and Yoko perform onstage with Frank Zappa and The Mothers Of Invention at the Fillmore East ballroom in New York. Edited highlights of the proceedings are included on their 1972 LP, 'Some Time In New York City' – on which John and Yoko cleverly claim composing credit for some of Zappa's music, notably a lengthy version of 'King Kong', over which they have improvised vocal parts. The peak of the 30-minute set is a commanding performance of The Olympics' R&B song, 'Well (Baby Please Don't Go)'.

EARLY JUNE
Lennon meets George Harrison at ABKCO's New York HQ, and invites him to play on his next LP sessions, set to begin late in the month. John and Yoko also meet political activists Jerry Rubin and Abbie Hoffman for the first time, in Washington Square Park. Rubin is subsequently appointed the couple's 'political adviser'.

Yoko records several avant-garde musical compositions with the Fluxus artist Joe Jones, and his Tone Deaf Music Co. Lennon nominally acts as producer.

Studio recordings:
'Airmale', 'You', 'Don't Count The Waves'.

18 JUNE
The Beatles' repackaging industry briefly rises from the dead, as 'The Early Years' brings together all their Hamburg studio recordings at budget price.

LATE JUNE
Back in Britain, Tittenhurst Park, the Lennons' home, is the venue as they begin recording what turns into the 'Imagine' LP. Many of the tracks on Yoko's 'Fly' LP are cut at the same time. The sessions are filmed intermittently for a semi-documentary movie designed to accompany the release of the two records.

Phil Spector acts as co-producer of the Lennon album, but steps graciously aside when Yoko's music is being performed. Likewise, George Harrison attends several sessions, but only plays on John's songs.

Studio recordings
(between now and mid-July):
'Imagine', 'Crippled Inside', 'Jealous Guy', 'It's So Hard', 'I Don't Wanna Be A Soldier', 'Gimme Some Truth', 'Oh My Love', 'How Do You Sleep', 'How', 'Oh Yoko', 'Well (Baby Please Don't Go)', 'I'm The Greatest', 'San Francisco Bay Blues', 'Mind Train', 'Mind Holes', 'Midsummer New York', 'O Wind', 'Mrs Lennon', 'Toilet Piece', 'Telephone Piece'.

84

START OF JULY
John and Yoko return to New York to supervise string and horn overdubs on their new recordings.

4 JULY
Legendary R&B saxophonist King Curtis adds his overdubs to two of Lennon's new songs.

Studio recordings:
'It's So Hard', 'I Don't Want To Be A Soldier'.

EARLY JULY
The Lennons return from New York to London for final vocal overdubs on the 'Imagine' album, and to continue work on their movie. They are accompanied by their new assistant, May Pang, picked from Allen Klein's ABKCO staff.
   At Tittenhurst Park, they shoot the memorable film sequence which accompanies the song 'Imagine', which begins with the Lennons trudging towards the house through the early morning mist, and climaxes with Lennon performing the song while Ono opens the shutters of their music room to the sunlight.
   Around this time, construction of the London International Hotel is completed, and so is the Lennon/Ono film *Erection*, documenting the process via a lengthy series of still photos. Yoko's recordings with Joe Jones are used on the soundtrack.

7 JULY
Apple in New York release 'God Save Us'/'Do The Oz' by Bill Elliott and the Elastic Oz Band.

13 JULY
In their bid to regain custody of Yoko's daughter Kyoko, the Lennons fly to the US Virgin Islands, where a judge grants them an order giving them the right to bring Kyoko up, as long as they grant reasonable access to Cox. Now all they have to do is find her: investigations suggest that she has been taken by her father to America.

MID-JULY
George Harrison invites both Paul McCartney and John Lennon to appear at his August

1 benefit concerts in New York to raise funds for the starving people of Bangladesh.

15 JULY
Back in London, after their eighth transatlantic flight in as many weeks, John and Yoko sign copies of the new paperback edition of Yoko's book, *Grapefruit*, at Selfridge's store.

16 JULY
'God Save Us' appears in Britain, but receives no airplay or press coverage, in an unspoken campaign to conceal Lennon's support of *Oz*. The media ignore a press conference to launch the record.

17 JULY
John and Yoko appear on the top-rated BBC TV chat show, *Parkinson*.

LATE JULY
The Lennons fly to New York for the Bangladesh concerts.

29 JULY
Lennon discovers that Harrison does not want Yoko Ono to appear at the benefit concerts. He concurs with this decision, until Yoko hears of the idea. The couple have a violent argument, and Lennon storms off to the airport, where he catches the first flight back to Europe.

1 AUGUST
George Harrison's benefit concerts for the starving people of Bangladesh take place without the involvement of the Lennons.

11 AUGUST
The Lennons march alongside anti-government protestors in London, decrying British policy towards Northern Ireland, and proclaiming their support "For the IRA, Against British Imperialism".

LATE AUGUST
Lennon briefly throws his public weight behind the campaign of the Upper Clydebank Shipbuilders in Scotland, who have been made redundant by the government and are refusing to leave their places of work.

3 SEPTEMBER
The Lennons leave London for New York; John will never return to Britain. Their departure is sparked by the need to pursue Yoko's ex-husband Tony Cox through the US courts, in order to gain custody of the couple's daughter, Kyoko. Lawyers advise Yoko that to secure her custody rights, she has to take up residence in America. John and Yoko take over a suite at the St. Regis Hotel.

John Lennon: "Yoko and I were forever coming and going to New York, so finally we decided it would be cheaper and more functional to actually live here."

5 SEPTEMBER
A film evening staged by London Art Spectrum at London's Alexander Palace sees the screening of five films by

the Lennons: *Cold Turkey, The Ballad Of Yoko And Yoko, Instant Karma, Give Peace A Chance* and *Up Your Legs Forever.*

9 SEPTEMBER
John's second solo album, 'Imagine', is released in the States, complete with the musical assault on Paul McCartney ('How Do You Sleep') and a postcard satirising the cover artwork of 'Ram'. McCartney had been pictured preparing a sheep for shearing on his LP; Lennon counters by parodying the pose with a pig. The album briefly reaches No. 1.

Lennon describes the record as " 'Plastic Ono Band' with sugar coating", and it is certainly a much less confrontational exercise than his previous album. It's also less focused, or if you prefer

more rounded, ranging from the confessional spirit of 'Jealous Guy' and the idealistic humanism of the title song, to the vicious self-indulgence of 'How Do You Sleep'. Eventually, though, the record's impact is diffused by the sheer popularity and durability of the song 'Imagine', which rapidly becomes an anthem not just for the counter-culture, but for any campaign group or religious sect seeking a suitably anodyne theme tune. The irony of a song that proclaims "Imagine no religion" being adopted almost as a Christmas carol by sections of the Church Of England would have amused Lennon, had he lived to see the day...

MID-SEPTEMBER
The Lennons continue their movie exploits at their suite at the St. Regis Hotel. One

morning, they make a film called *Clock*, which consists of the hands of a clock turning through 60 minutes: on the soundtrack is Lennon performing a selection of rock'n'roll oldies (plus an early stab at 'New York City') on acoustic guitar, while Yoko Ono makes phone calls.

Also at this time, Lennon writes two unremarkable new songs, 'JJ' (the tune of which is later hijacked for 'Angela') and 'Shoeshine' (pilfered in 1973 for the lyrics to 'Meat City').

They also continue to film segments for the *Imagine* movie, featuring guests like Fred Astaire, Dick Cavett and Phil Spector.

Dick Cavett: "I met them in their hotel room on a rainy day. John pulled out a 16mm film camera and said, 'Could I take a little thing of you?' It later ended up in a movie of his."

20 SEPTEMBER

Yoko's double-album, 'Fly', appears in the US. It features two Plastic Ono Band B-sides, soundtrack recordings from two of the Lennons' films, and several new songs. These range from 'Mrs Lennon', a mournful ballad which comments on the way in which her individuality has been overshadowed by John's fame, to 'Mind Train', a remarkably intense and ambitious 17-minute rock outing. Despite its range and adventurousness, it can only register at No. 199 in the album chart.

23 SEPTEMBER

John and Yoko appear on ABC-TV's *The Dick Cavett Show*, previewing their *Imagine* and *Fly* movies. Lennon walks on stage with a cigarette in his hand, points to it, and says: "See, Janov? It didn't work." Arthur Janov's Primal Therapy is supposed to have cured Lennon of all his addictions.

29 SEPTEMBER

'Mrs Lennon' is selected as potentially the most radio-friendly item on 'Fly', and released as a US single.

OCTOBER

In *Melody Maker*, two readers write a letter questioning Lennon's political principles; he replies with an open letter, stating: "I personally have had enough of Apple/Ascot and all other properties which tie me down, mentally and physically – I intend to cash in my chips as soon as I can – and be FREE!"

8 OCTOBER

Neatly missing Lennon's birthday, Apple release the 'Imagine' album in Britain. Meanwhile, the Lennons stage a press conference in Syracuse, upstate New York, to mark the opening of Yoko's art exhibition the next day. They also join a demonstration by Onondaga Indians against the building of a freeway through their reservation.

9 OCTOBER

This Is Not Here, an exhibition of art by Yoko Ono and her friends, opens at the Everson Museum in Syracuse, and runs until October 27. Besides contributions from the Lennons, the exhibition includes non-stop screenings of many of their films, notably *Clock*. The theme of the exhibition is water, and many of Yoko's friends and other celebrities have contributed pieces which can be filled with liquid before being put on display.

During the day, Lennon and Ono are interviewed for the first time by Elliot Mintz, a DJ and journalist who will later become a close friend.

That night, Lennon celebrates his 31st birthday with a party at their hotel, which develops into a ramshackle jam session with guests like Phil Spector, Allen Ginsberg and Ringo Starr. Lennon ensures that, as usual, the evening's fun is recorded for posterity. There is one vaguely positive result from the frolics: John writes a new song, the overtly radical and simplistic 'Attica State'.

11 OCTOBER

The title track of the 'Imagine' album is released as an American single, having proved to be by far the most popular song on the record. It reaches No. 3 in the charts, and is accepted as an instant standard. The single isn't released in Britain until 1975, however, delaying the song's full impact there for another four years.

14 OCTOBER

The Lennons are interviewed on the TV show *Free Time*. Around this time, they also meet rock journalist Robert Christgau, having read one of his *Village Voice* articles about them.

MID-OCTOBER

Street singer David Peel is introduced to Lennon after one of his regular Washington Square Park gigs. John and Yoko join Peel on a subsequent occasion, and are moved on by the police. Lennon is so enthralled by his new-found street credibility that he offers

American Editor Chris Charlesworth, to whom he lets slip his first public hints that his marriage is on the rocks. Charlesworth and Lennon met for the first time the previous evening at the Rainbow Bar & Grill on Sunset Strip.

29 OCTOBER
The US single 'Mind Games' is Lennon's first release since the spring of 1972. It stalls at No. 18. On the flipside is 'Meat City', a beefy rocker with some mysterious vocal segments. Play the single backwards, and one of those spoken sections reveals the intriguing clue: "Check the album". Try the LP version of the same song, and the backwards segment announces: "Fuck a pig".

31 OCTOBER
The FBI replies to Lennon's allegations in typically obtuse style: "Review failed to indicate that Lennon or premises in which he had proprietary interest have been subjected to any lawful electronic surveillance".

EARLY NOVEMBER
The Spector sessions collapse, in a haze of alcohol, drugs and general confusion. Lennon and

Pang decide to spend a few days in San Francisco, but the night before their trip, John tells May their affair is over. She returns to New York. Lennon has a one-night stand with a back-up singer, then returns to Harold Seider's apartment.

2 NOVEMBER
Apple release, but hardly bother to promote, the new Yoko Ono album, 'Feeling The Space' in the States. It comes into direct competition with Lennon's new record, 'Mind Games', only this time the collision isn't masterminded by Lennon, as it had been in 1970.

'Mind Games' reveals the emptiness at the heart of Lennon's creative and personal life in 1973. Its music is often uninspired, and its lyrics reflect disillusionment rather than John's usual optimism. "It's just an album," Lennon admits in one interview, "it's rock and roll at different speeds. There's no very deep message about it. The only reason I make albums is because you're supposed to."

Completing a full release schedule for Apple's New York office, Ringo Starr's 'Ringo' LP also appears on this day – with Lennon's song 'I'm The Greatest' as the lead cut. 'Ringo' reaches

No. 2, 'Mind Games' only No. 9.

Meanwhile, Apple is rocked by the news that business manager Allen Klein has been sacked, and that Lennon, Harrison and Starr are suing Klein's ABKCO company, claiming that it has withheld royalty payments. The dispute effectively kills Apple as anything beyond a marketing and financial organisation for The Beatles; no new artists are signed to the label after this point.

9 NOVEMBER
Apple's British office makes its priorities clear, delaying Lennon's LP for a week so that it can rush-release the 'Ringo' album – and Yoko's 'Run, Run, Run' single.

16 NOVEMBER
British release date for the 'Mind Games' single and album.

20 NOVEMBER
Lennon writes an inimitably punctuated letter to ex-Beatles press officer Derek Taylor: "im in L.ostA.rsoles, for no real reason, staying all over LOU gold disk ADLERs' ... it's free which always impressed me. yoko and me are in hell, but im gonna change it, probably this very day."

23 NOVEMBER
'Feeling The Space' finally makes the UK release sheets.

DECEMBER
Lennon continues his campaign to save Michael X from the death penalty, writing a personal letter to the family of Trinidad prime minister Eric Williams.

He also invites May Pang to return to California, ostensibly to help look after his son Julian and ex-wife Cynthia, who are due for a post-Christmas visit. When she returns, the Phil Spector sessions resume, punctuated by the usual round of erratic behaviour: one night, Spector lets off a handgun in the studio; on another, Lennon, Pang, Harry Nilsson and Cher end up at the *Playboy* mansion owned by Hugh Hefner. But Spector and Lennon do manage to collaborate on an original song, 'Here We Go Again'.

Studio recordings:
'Here We Go Again', 'Sweet Little Sixteen', 'You Can't Catch Me', 'Just Because', 'To Know You Is To Love You', 'My Baby Left Me'.

MID-DECEMBER
'The Jim Keltner Fan Club' – alias many of the musicians from the Lennon/Spector sessions – convene at the Record Plant

93

without the erratic Phil. Lennon ends up as producer for the night, while Mick Jagger performs the Seventies soul hit 'Too Many Cooks'.

LATE DECEMBER

Cynthia and Julian Lennon arrive in California; the extended Lennon family visits Disneyland. According to May Pang, Cynthia tells Lennon that she wants to have another child with him; Lennon tells her that a doctor has told him he is sterile.

1974

JANUARY

It is reported that John has written directly to the Queen to ask for a royal pardon for his drugs conviction from 1968 – which would immediately solve his immigration battle. The Queen is apparently not forthcoming.

EARLY JANUARY

Lennon, May Pang, Cynthia, Jesse Ed Davis and Jim Keltner attend an Ann Peebles show at the Troubadour in LA. Lennon over-indulges as usual, and ends up with a Kotex sanitary napkin stuck to his forehead.

A waitress refuses to serve him any more alcohol. "Don't you know who I am?" he asks her. "You're the asshole with a Kotex on your head," she replies. Later that night, Lennon knocks Jesse Ed Davis unconscious, assaults Pang, wrecks the apartment, and has to deal with a visit from local police officers, replying to accounts from neighbours of gunfire in the house.

MID-JANUARY

Phil Spector requests that Lennon accompanies him to his divorce hearing; the pair argue, and the album sessions are abruptly cancelled. Lennon and Pang return to New York, where John is greeted with the news that Yoko wants a divorce. He also attends a series of meetings to discuss the settlement of the dispute between the ex-Beatles and Allen Klein.

FEBRUARY

Lennon sells the piano on which he has written many songs, to raise funds for Michael X's legal campaign.

18 FEBRUARY

John and May Pang visit the Dakota for a 20-minute visit on Yoko's 41st birthday; tension is rife, but all talk of a divorce has subsided.

20 FEBRUARY

Lennon and Pang return to Los Angeles. They attempt to contact Phil Spector to resume the recording sessions, but are told that he has suffered a car accident, and is convalescing.

1 MARCH

The legal battle against the Immigration Service continues, as Lennon returns to court to appeal against the government's latest victory in their campaign to deport him.

EARLY MARCH

At a Hollywood party, Lennon is introduced to David Bowie by actress Elizabeth Taylor.

12 MARCH

Lennon and Harry Nilsson attend a nightclub performance by the comedy team The Smothers Brothers at the Troubadour in Los Angeles. Out of their minds on Brandy Alexanders, the pair heckle the Smothers, and are eventually asked to leave. The incident turns into a fracas, as Lennon lashes out at those who are escorting him off the premises, and reportedly hits a waitress – though her subsequent legal case against him is dropped.

Tommy Smothers: "It was a big Hollywood opening. During our first set I heard someone yelling about pigs... it was fairly disgusting. I couldn't figure out who it was. But I knew Harry and John were there. The heckling got so bad that our show was going downhill rapidly. No-one cared, because it was just a happening anyway, but there was a scuffle going on and we stopped the show.

"Flowers came the next day apologizing. My wife ended up with Lennon's glasses because

of the punches that were thrown. Then he went outside 'cause he was still angry and kicked the car parker."

John Lennon: "I got drunk and shouted – it was my first night on Brandy Alexanders, that's brandy and milk, folks. I was with Harry Nilsson, who didn't get as much coverage as me – the bum. He encouraged me. So I was drunk – when it's Errol Flynn, the showbiz writers say, 'Those were the days, when men were men'. When I do it, I'm a bum."

13 MARCH

Lennon and Nilsson send flowers and a note of apology to The Smothers Brothers, while the local press play up the 'ex-Beatle in drunken fight' angle for all it's worth.

LATE MARCH

With the Spector project apparently on permanent hold, Nilsson and Lennon decide to direct their rampant energies towards the making of a new Nilsson album, which Lennon will produce.

After a drunken evening at the Beverly Wilshire Hotel, Lennon apparently attempts to strangle May Pang as she tries to prevent him drinking; Nilsson loosens his fingers from around her neck. When the frolics continue outdoors, the Lennon contingent is politely asked to leave the hotel. They reassemble at a rented home on Santa Monica Beach.

EARLY APRIL

Recording sessions for Nilsson's LP begin at the Record Plant West. Hard drinkers from around the world, like Ringo Starr, Jesse Ed Davis and Keith Moon, assemble for the party.

The first night's session is enlivened by an alcohol-fuelled jam session between Lennon and guests Paul McCartney and Stevie Wonder. The last musical collaboration between John and Paul proves to be less than historic in artistic terms. The sessions continue for several weeks, until Nilsson begins to suffer severe throat problems that result in him coughing up blood while he's

singing. Lennon decides that Nilsson needs to be removed from the hedonistic climate of California, and that the sessions should be resumed in New York. John insists that May Pang remain in Santa Monica; as usual, she obeys.

MAY

Transplanted from West to East, the Nilsson sessions resume at the Record Plant in New York. May Pang rejoins Lennon mid-month at the Pierre Hotel.

1 MAY

A US district court rules against Lennon in his appeal against the Immigration Service's appeal.

17/18 MAY

With Harry Nilsson, Lennon takes part in the annual 'March Of Dimes' charity event in Philadelphia, acting as a guest DJ for station WFIL-FM during both days.

JUNE

Harry Nilsson's 'Pussy Cats' album is completed.

Having not been in contact with Lennon since the collapse of their sessions the previous December, Phil Spector unexpectedly delivers the tapes of their collaboration to Lennon's office. Unwilling to face listening to the aural chaos, John puts them to one side and attempts to forget about them. Meanwhile, he begins taping home demos of a set of new material, including 'Whatever Gets You Through The Night', 'Goodnight Vienna', 'So Long', 'Move Over Ms L', 'What You Got' and 'Surprise Surprise'.

13 JUNE

Following a Who concert at Madison Square Garden, Lennon and May Pang are visited in their Pierre Hotel suite by Who drummer Keith Moon and *Melody Maker*'s American Editor Chris Charlesworth. All John has to offer his guests is a bottle of extremely expensive vintage red wine, a gift from Allen Klein. Despite Moon's eagerness to taste it, John cautions his guests by pointing out that Klein was in litigation with him at the time, and may

Elton John: "I said to John, 'I'd love to record one of your songs. Which one would you like me to do?' And he said, 'No one's ever done "Lucy In The Sky With Diamonds", no one's ever recorded that'."

have good reason to want to poison him. After some discussion, Charlesworth is elected as 'taster'. The wine was fine.

8 JULY
Lennon's masterful arrangement of Jimmy Cliff's 'Many Rivers To Cross' becomes the lead US single from his production of Harry Nilsson's upcoming album.

13 JULY
John holds rehearsal sessions for his upcoming album at Record Plant in New York.

18 JULY
More drama in the immigration case: Lennon's October 1973 appeal is denied, and another order to leave within 60 days is made. Lennon files another appeal.

LATE JULY
The recording of the 'Walls And Bridges' album begins at the Record Plant. Lennon also sends a demo tape of 'Goodnight Vienna' to Ringo Starr in California.

AUGUST
Julian and Cynthia Lennon visit John and May at their New York apartment. Julian stays for

several days, during which time Paul and Linda McCartney also pay a call. Julian and John briefly jam in the studio, on a version of Lee Dorsey's 'Ya Ya'. Another regular visitor is Elton John, whom Lennon persuades to help out with the album sessions. Elton adds vocals to two tunes, 'Whatever Gets You Through The Night' and 'Surprise, Surprise'.

Studio recordings:
'Going Down On Love', 'Whatever Gets You Through The Night', 'Old Dirt Road', 'What You Got', 'Bless You', 'Scared', 'No. 9 Dream', 'Surprise Surprise', 'Steel And Glass', 'Beef Jerky', 'Nobody Loves You When You're Down And Out', 'Ya Ya', 'Move Over Ms L'.

Meanwhile, Yoko Ono undertakes her first concert tour of Japan, shocking polite society with her on-stage demeanour and frankness in interviews.

19 AUGUST
Nilsson's 'Pussy Cats' album is released in the States, to lukewarm response from an audience who seem to want lush ballads from the artist, rather than the frequently anarchic, but still compelling, rock'n'roll supervised by producer John Lennon. The album only makes No. 60 in the chart.

23 AUGUST
Looking out the window of his New York apartment, Lennon glimpses a UFO.

LATE AUGUST
Having completed 'Walls And Bridges', Lennon jets to California with May Pang for another Ringo Starr session. As he had the previous year, he's knocked off a song for his former colleague, 'Goodnight Vienna'; and once again he takes control of the session, laying down his own rendition of the song as a guide for Ringo. He also arranges and plays acoustic guitar on Ringo's cover of The Platters' hit 'Only You'. From there, Lennon and Pang fly north to Caribou Ranch studios, where John collaborates with Elton John on a version of The Beatles' 'Lucy In The Sky With Diamonds'. For the flipside, Elton respectfully tackles Lennon's 'One Day At A Time'.
    Elton John: "I said to John, 'I'd love to record one of your songs. Which one would you like me to do?' And he said, 'No one's ever done "Lucy In The Sky With Diamonds", no one's ever recorded that'."

Studio recordings:
'Only You', 'Goodnight Vienna', 'Lucy In The Sky With Diamonds', 'One Day At A Time'.

30 AUGUST
UK release date for 'Pussy Cats'.

31 AUGUST
Lennon appears in a federal court to claim that he has been denied the right to remain in the USA on purely political grounds, because the Nixon administration feared in 1972 that he would campaign against the President's re-election.

12 SEPTEMBER
The issue of *Melody Maker* which goes on sale on this day features an interview with musician Todd Rundgren, who lambasts John Lennon as a hypocrite.

13 SEPTEMBER
'Many Rivers To Cross' belatedly appears in the UK

23 SEPTEMBER
'Whatever Gets You Through The Night', a duet with Elton John, becomes Lennon's first US single of the year – and his first American No. 1 single as well.

26 SEPTEMBER
Three days after the single, the 'Walls And Bridges' album hits the stores, in its cut-up sleeve covered in paintings by the pre-teen Lennon. In the wake of the single, it too reaches No. 1.

But one listener isn't happy: publisher Morris Levy, who notes that Lennon has recorded just one of his songs, a brief snippet of 'Ya Ya', rather than the three which Lennon had promised as settlement to their legal dispute a year before.

The album is dismissed by Lennon in 1980 as the work of "a semi-sick craftsman", but its comfortable command of contemporary soul styles, its adult recognition of the conflicting demands of his relationships with Yoko and May Pang, and its handling of both pleasure and pain, mark it out as his finest post-1971 work. His later comments seem to reflect the official John and Yoko line that he was incapable of producing decent work without her. In fact, his period apart from Yoko is one of the most prolific periods of his working life.

Meanwhile, Lennon replies to Todd Rundgren's criticism of two weeks earlier with a conciliatory 'open letter' in *Melody Maker*.

27 SEPTEMBER
During a frantic week of publicity for 'Walls And Bridges', Lennon visits radio station KHJ-AM in Los Angeles to guest on the morning show. Sounding as if he's been feeding off pure adrenalin for a week, Lennon takes phone-in calls from bemused listeners who are unable to keep pace with his wired, surreal conversation.

28 SEPTEMBER
Twenty-four hours later, on the other side of America, a considerably more relaxed Lennon is Dennis Elsas's guest on WNEW-FM in New York. He's met Elsas at the Record Plant, and received a vague invitation to come down and appear on his show whenever he wants. He arrives with a batch of his favourite oldies, like Ritchie Barrett's 'Some Other Guy' and Derek Martin's 'Daddy Rolling Stone', and also joins whole-heartedly into the business of being a DJ, romping through commercials and station links, tongue firmly in cheek.

OCTOBER
Yoko Ono issues a new single in Japan, with no help from Lennon. 'Yume O Motou (Let's Have A Dream)' is backed by the original version of 'It Happened', which is reissued in eerily modified form in 1981.

EARLY OCTOBER
John's back in California, and on the radio again – this time on KSAN-FM in San Francisco, with veteran DJ Tom Donahue. In a cultured discussion, the pair talk about record production, before Lennon unveils the unissued track he produced for Mick Jagger, 'Too Many Cooks'.

1 OCTOBER
Lennon's heavily-echoed, playful and chaotic arrangement of Bob Dylan's 'Subterranean Homesick Blues' is issued as the second US single from Nilsson's 'Pussy Cats' LP.

4 OCTOBER
UK release date for 'Whatever Gets You Through The Night' and 'Walls And Bridges'.

8 OCTOBER
Morris Levy meets Lennon at the Club Cavallero in New York to discuss a solution to their legal dispute. Levy later claims that during this meeting, Lennon agrees to let Levy market John's next album via his mail-order label, Adam VIII Records. Lennon counters by saying that the idea was only discussed, not agreed.

Either way, it is decided that Lennon will revive the 'Oldies But Goldies' project he'd abandoned when the Spector sessions collapsed at the end of 1973. He decides to rescue as many songs as possible from the tapes Spector has delivered, and then add another batch of rock'n'roll favourites from sessions later this month.

MID-OCTOBER
Morris Levy's upstate New York farm is the location for the rehearsal sessions for Lennon's oldies album. The so-called 'May Pang Tapes', issued on various bootlegs, date from this weekend's work.

21-25 OCTOBER
Basking in the commercial success of his latest single and album, Lennon feels sufficiently confident to return to the traumatic 'Oldies But Goldies' project he had begun with Phil Spector the previous autumn. He hires the 'Walls & Bridges' band once again, and steers them through a week of professional and occasionally inspired sessions. He also overdubs new vocals on three of the Spector tracks, effectively bidding farewell to the record business with his mumbled comments over the fade-out of 'Just Because'.

Studio recordings:
'Be-Bop-A-Lula', 'Stand By Me', 'Rip It Up', 'Ready Teddy', 'Ain't That A Shame', 'Do You Wanna Dance', 'Slippin' And Slidin' ', 'Peggy Sue', 'Bring It On Home To Me', 'Send Me Some Lovin' ', 'Ya Ya', 'Sweet Little Sixteen', 'Be My Baby', 'You Can't Catch Me'.

NOVEMBER
The latest issue of Andy Warhol's *Interview* magazine contains a Lennon 'self-interview'.

EARLY NOVEMBER
Lennon delivers Morris Levy a set of the rough mixes of his 'Oldies' album. Yoko Ono supposedly engages a Tarot Card reader, to help her regain John's affection.

1 NOVEMBER
Lennon makes another legal move in his immigration battle, requesting the right to question specific government officials about their campaign to deport him on political grounds.

11 NOVEMBER
John's acoustic guitar is the backbone for Ringo Starr's new US single, 'Only You (And You Alone)', which reaches No. 6.

12 NOVEMBER
After years of media controversy and outright hostility, Lennon's popularity in the USA is fully restored, as both 'Whatever Gets You Through The Night' and 'Walls And Bridges' both reach No. 1 on the US charts.

14 NOVEMBER
Lennon, Pang and Ono attend the opening of *Sgt. Pepper's Lonely Hearts Club Band On The Road*, a Broadway musical based around The Beatles' music. Lennon vanishes after the show; when Pang phones Ono to enquire after his whereabouts, Yoko tells her: "I'm thinking of taking him back".

15 NOVEMBER
Alongside 'Only You', Ringo's 'Goodnight Vienna' album is also released in Britain – with a throwaway title track written by Lennon around a piece of vintage Liverpool slang.

Issued on the same day is Elton John's 'Lucy In The Sky With Diamonds', on which Lennon sings and plays guitar. Lennon also performs on the flipside, his 'Mind Games' song 'One Day At A Time'.

18 NOVEMBER
US release date for 'Goodnight Vienna' and 'Lucy In The Sky With Diamonds', which makes No. 1 in the first week of 1975.

24 NOVEMBER
Elton John has made Lennon promise that if 'Whatever Gets You Through The Night' gets to No. 1, John will join him on stage to perform the song. Now he calls in his IOU, and persuades John to attend rehearsals for his upcoming New York gig.

25 NOVEMBER
Johnny Winter exposes Lennon's song 'Rock'n'Roll People' to the outside world for the first time, on his 'John Dawson Winter III' album. Lennon had given Winter a tape of his own recording of the tune, from the 'Walls And Bridges' sessions.

28 NOVEMBER
Some 20,000 Elton John fans at Madison Square Garden in New York are witness to John Lennon's final concert appearance, as he joins Elton for the encores of his performance. The pair perform exuberant, though hardly flawless, renditions of 'Whatever Gets You Through The Night', 'Lucy In The Sky With Diamonds' and 'I Saw Her Standing There' – which Lennon introduces as "a song by an old

estranged fiancé of mine, called Paul". The audience reception is tumultuous.

Elton John: "It was an occasion where grown men, even Scottish road managers who'd seen it all, cried. I've never seen anybody get an ovation like that. When he walked on stage, it shook him. He was physically sick when he came on stage that night, he was so scared. But he kept his bargain." After the show, Lennon and Yoko Ono meet backstage. The couple later claim that Lennon hadn't known Yoko would be at the show, and that this is the moment when their romance blossomed for the second time. May Pang, however, counters that Ono had been hassling Lennon for days to make sure she had good seats for the concert. After the show, she says, Lennon and Ono merely chatted briefly: "He didn't even say goodnight to Yoko".

9 DECEMBER
Another US Nilsson single produced by Lennon: the singalong 'Loop De Loop', again from the 'Pussy Cats' LP.

Lennon crops up as a guest during half-time on ABC-TV's live transmission of *Monday Night Football*, and is interviewed by sportscaster Howard Cosell.

14 DECEMBER
Lennon and George Harrison meet at the Plaza Hotel in New York. Lennon offers to join Harrison at his Madison Square Garden show later that week; Harrison responds bitterly: "Where were you when I needed you?"

15 DECEMBER
John and George repair their quarrel; John attends George's show at the Nassau Coliseum on Long Island.

16 DECEMBER
Lennon follows up his US No. 1 hit with 'Whatever Gets You Through The Night' by issuing 'No. 9 Dream' as a single. Suitably, it peaks at No. 9 in the chart.

19 DECEMBER
George Harrison finally invites John to join him on stage at Madison Square Garden. Lennon, Harrison and McCartney are due to sign the official dissolution of The Beatles' business partnership that afternoon, but Lennon backs out of the deal at the last minute. In response, Harrison tells Pang: "Tell him I started this tour on my own and I'll end it on my own."

20 DECEMBER
Lennon meets with Lee Eastman, Paul McCartney's father-in-law, in an attempt to break the impasse in The Beatles' business negotiations. Eastman pressures Lennon to sign, but their meeting ends when John learns that Harrison has mellowed since the previous night, and has invited him to attend the end-of-tour party. John and George also agree to be interviewed together briefly by KHJ-FM radio in Los Angeles.

1975

2 JANUARY
Judge Richard Owen rules in Lennon's favour, and says that he should be allowed to interview Immigration Service officials, and inspect their files, to discover whether political motives had indeed played a part in their campaign to have Lennon deported.

EARLY JANUARY
John takes Julian for a rare visit to see Yoko at the Dakota.

9 JANUARY
On a trip to Disneyworld in Florida with Julian, Lennon overcomes his qualms about the deal severing The Beatles' business dealings, and signs the required document. 'The Beatles & Company', the partnership tying Lennon, McCartney, Harrison and Starr as a legal entity, is thus formally dissolved. From this point on, The Beatles exist only as a memory.

top: John with Yoko at
the Grammy Awards;
below: The Dakota Building;
main picture: John with Sean
and Yoko.

John Lennon: "This last year has been extraordinary for me personally. I got such a shock that the impact hasn't come through. It has to do with age and God knows what else. But I'm through it and it's '75 and I feel better and I'm sitting here and not lying in some weird place with a hangover. I feel like I've been on Sinbad's voyage and I've battled all those monsters and I've got back."

MID-JANUARY

David Bowie invites Lennon to his final sessions for the 'Young Americans' album, to contribute to a cover of The Beatles' 'Across The Universe'. During a jam session, Lennon, Bowie and guitarist Carlos Alomar stumble on a cute funk riff which turns into 'Fame'.

Studio recordings:
'Across The Universe', 'Fame'.

LATE JANUARY

Lennon has at least two songs ready for his next album project at this stage – a tribute to playwright Tennessee Williams, suitably titled 'Tennessee', and the playful 'Popcorn'.

31 JANUARY

UK release date for Lennon's 'No. 9 Dream' single, and for a last attempt at a hit from Nilsson's 'Pussy Cats', via Lennon's languorous, Spectoresque arrangement of 'Save The Last Dance For Me'.

8 FEBRUARY

Morris Levy begins a TV advertising campaign for an album entitled 'Roots: John Lennon Sings The Rock'n'Roll Hits'. It consists of the rough mix of Lennon's 'Oldies' LP, as given to Levy the previous November. Advance news of this release spurs Lennon into okaying the release of the 'official' LP from the sessions, 'Rock 'N' Roll'.

13 FEBRUARY

Lennon appears – uninvited, but very welcome – as guest DJ for three hours on Scott Muni's WNEW-FM show in New York. He brings with him an advance copy of his 'Rock 'N' Roll' LP, and discusses the reasons why he chose to record each track.

MID-FEBRUARY

Yoko contacts Lennon repeatedly to persuade him to try a revolutionary form of hypnosis to help him quit smoking. Lennon initially rejects her advances, but then agrees to return to the Dakota for one session. When he hasn't returned that night, May Pang phones to speak to him, and is told by Yoko that he's too tired to talk.

Three days later, Lennon and Pang meet at their dentist's office. "Yoko has allowed me to come home", he tells her. "Yoko knows I still love you.

She's allowed me to continue to see you." The couple meet regularly through to the end of March, when Pang is dispatched to England on Apple business.

Around this time, Yoko becomes pregnant.

17 FEBRUARY
Less than five months after 'Walls And Bridges', Lennon releases another album, 'Rock 'N' Roll' – rush-released in the States to counter the effect of the TV advertising for the 'unauthorised' mail-order LP 'Roots'. Sales haven't been hit too badly, as 'Rock 'N' Roll' reaches No. 6.

20 FEBRUARY
In a New York court, Judge Griesa orders that 'Roots' should be withdrawn from sale, pending final legal

judgement. In fact, Capitol have already pressured TV stations not to take adverts for the 'unofficial' album.

21 FEBRUARY
'Rock 'N' Roll' is also issued in Britain, where 'Roots' has not been available.

24 FEBRUARY
Three months after the event, Elton John issues his live duet of 'I Saw Her Standing There' with Lennon, from Madison Square Garden, on the back of his 'Philadelphia Freedom' single.

26 FEBRUARY
"Feel great," Lennon writes of his reunion with Yoko to old friend Derek Taylor, "like a chicken wots got its ead back."

28 FEBRUARY
UK release date for the Elton John single.

1 MARCH
John appears at the televised Grammy Awards ceremony as a guest presenter. Yoko is also present, their first public appearance together in more than 18 months.

6 MARCH
"The separation didn't work out", Lennon reveals in a press release to announce to the world his reunion with Yoko Ono. The couple have been undergoing a liquid fast, followed by a strict regimen of macrobiotic food. During this period, they discover that Yoko has become pregnant – as promised by the acupuncturist who has been supervising their diets since their reunion.

9 MARCH
Lennon is interviewed by Pete Hamill for *Rolling Stone* magazine.

John Lennon: "This last year has been extraordinary for me personally. I got such a shock that the impact hasn't come through. It has to do with age and God knows what else. But I'm through it and it's '75 and I feel better and I'm sitting here and not lying in some weird place with a hangover. I feel like I've been on Sinbad's voyage and I've battled all those monsters and I've got back."

10 MARCH
Lennon attempts to rival 'Philadelphia Freedom' in the singles chart by releasing his cover of 'Stand By Me' from the 'Rock 'N' Roll' album; it reaches No. 20. The track, built around a

similar acoustic guitar riff to Ringo Starr's 'Only You', is backed by an out-take from the sessions, Lennon's 'Move Over Ms L'. The song sounds like a farewell to Yoko Ono, ironically issued just weeks after the couple have reunited.

On the same day, another record featuring Lennon reaches American stores – David Bowie's 'Young Americans' LP, with Lennon singing and co-writing 'Fame', and playing guitar on his own 'Across The Universe'.

MID-MARCH

BBC TV's Bob Harris interviews Lennon for *The Old Grey Whistle Test*. To accompany their conversation, Lennon is filmed in the Record Plant East, singing new vocal tracks over the released versions of 'Stand By Me' and 'Slippin' And Slidin'. He also slips in a brief extract from Labelle's 'Lady Marmalade', though this isn't broadcast, and takes the opportunity to say hello to his relatives in England.

20 MARCH

The Lennons celebrate their sixth wedding anniversary with a renewal of vows in a mock-Druidic ceremony at the Dakota.

28 MARCH

Bowie's 'Young Americans' LP, with its Lennon guest appearances, is released in Britain.

18 APRIL

To coincide with Lennon's appearance on *The Old Grey Whistle Test*, 'Stand By Me' belatedly appears as a UK single.

MID-APRIL

Having returned from London, May Pang meets Lennon again, and they continue their affair for the next five months, albeit less frequently than in the past.

28 APRIL

Lennon and his immigration dispute lawyer, Leon Wildes, appear on Tom Snyder's NBC-TV chat show *Tomorrow*, to discuss the progress of his case. John manages to remain witty and polite despite the inanities spouted by his host. It is his last major TV interview.

EARLY SUMMER

Lennon sends another missive to Derek Taylor: "I meself have decided to be or not to be for a coupla years? Boredom set in... how many backbeats are there? I ask meself... Am writing 'in his own wife' part ninety. It's good but I dread dealing with those assholes..."

2 JUNE

Lennon's song 'Goodnight Vienna' is the final choice of US single from Ringo Starr's album of the same name. Issued on the same day is David Bowie's 'Fame' single, written with Lennon and guitarist Earl Slick; it becomes the third Lennon-related No. 1 single in less than a year.

13 JUNE

Supported by a group dubbed 'Etcetera', all of whom are wearing 'two-faced' masks, Lennon makes a final TV appearance as a performing musician, on the show *A Salute To Sir Lew Grade*. His three-song set – comprising 'Slippin' And Slidin' ', 'Stand By Me' and 'Imagine' – is part of a belated settlement of the publishing dispute over material co-written by Lennon and Ono which had delayed the UK release of several Lennon records in the early Seventies. The bejewelled audience seem rather bemused by the sight of a long-haired, red-jumpsuited ex-Beatle singing about "a brotherhood and sisterhood of man".

19 JUNE

Taking the legal offensive, Lennon files suit against ex-Attorneys General John Mitchell and Richard Kleindienst, claiming that they blocked his visa applications for political reasons.

13 JULY

The court focus switches from immigration matters to Lennon's battle with Morris Levy, over the 'Roots' LP. Judge Griesa decides that both sides should pay the other damages, with Lennon coming out on top.

John Lennon: "The reason I fought this was to discourage ridiculous suits like this. They didn't think I'd show or that I'd fight it. They thought I'd just settle, but I won't."

18 JULY

'Fame' is released as a UK single.

LATE SUMMER

Lennon contacts his half-sister Julia for the first time since he moved to America. The siblings maintain regular phone contact for the next couple of years, before losing touch again.

SEPTEMBER

"I ain't in a hurry to sign with anyone... or do anything," Lennon writes to Derek Taylor. "Am enjoying my pregnancy... thinking time... whats it all about time too. I have some beautifull songs... but (for the

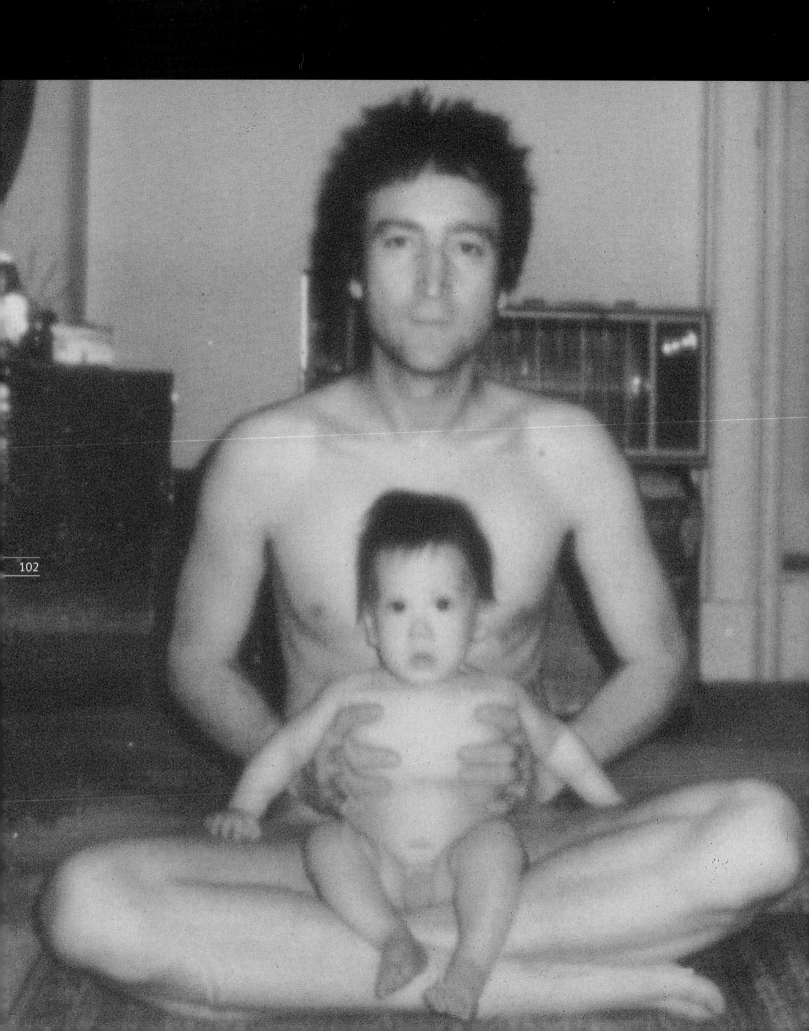

first time) dont feel an INCREDIBLE URGE... I'll outlive the bastards in more ways than one (whatever their age)... My head and body are as clear as a bell... some nice window pane... and some incredibely LEGAL MUSHROOMS. Have finished writing a NEW BOOK... same style (almost...) have to edit... but dont feel like dealing with ASSHOLES."

7 OCTOBER
Victory for John Lennon against the US government: an appeal court annuls the original deportation order against him, and insists that the Immigration Service reconsider his request for full resident status. In a clear signal to the Service, the court notes: "Lennon's four-year battle to remain in our country is a testimony to his faith in that American dream".

9 OCTOBER
A momentous week continues: on Lennon's 35th birthday, and seven years after their first attempt, 42-year-old Yoko Ono finally delivers a son in New York. The birth is by Caesarian section, after Yoko goes into convulsions during labour. "I've always wanted to shake your hand," says the surgeon to Lennon; "Fuck off", John replies brusquely, "and save Yoko's life".

The Lennons name the 8lb. 10 ozs. boy Sean Taro Ono Lennon. "Don't brand the child," complains John's Aunt Mimi when she is told of her grandson's name. The birth of his son finally forces Lennon to cease his affair with May Pang.

21 OCTOBER
After two weeks of intense medical care, Yoko and Sean are finally allowed home from hospital.

24 OCTOBER
Though the symbolism is not apparent at the time, Lennon draws a thick line under his musical career by issuing a retrospective album, 'Shaved Fish', and allowing 'Imagine' to appear as a UK single for the first time. 'Shaved Fish'

collects together all John's US solo singles, though only a small section of 'Give Peace A Chance' is used to open the record, while an equally brief clip of the song, as performed at the 1972 One To One concerts, is the final track.

In the States, the LP reaches No. 12.

29 DECEMBER
Black activist Michael X is hanged on a murder charge in Trinidad. Repeated appeals for clemency from the Lennons are ignored by the Trinidadian government.

1976

1 JANUARY
Elliot Mintz, who continues in close contact with the Lennons, interviews John, while baby Sean gurgles contentedly in the background.

5 JANUARY
Former Beatles aide and close friend of Lennon, Mal Evans, is shot dead by Los Angeles police, after he has apparently taken his girlfriend hostage and threatened her with a gun. When he hears the news, Lennon weeps.

MID-JANUARY
Lennon records a home demo of 'Mucho Mungo' – a song he's already cut in 1974 with Harry Nilsson – for no apparent purpose. He also concocts another song for Ringo, 'Cookin' (In The Kitchen Of Love)'.

26 JANUARY
The Beatles' nine-year recording contract with EMI, which has tied them collectively and individually since 1967, finally expires. Three of the group immediately negotiate new deals; Lennon chooses to remain a free agent.

FEBRUARY
Capitol Records executives write to Lennon, asking him when they can expect his next album of new material. Lennon doesn't respond.

Starting around this time,

and continuing for the next 18 months, Lennon and May Pang meet sporadically to resume their affair.

5 MARCH
EMI spark an instant revival of Beatlemania when they reissue all 22 of the group's original UK singles, and add a new release to the catalogue: 'Yesterday'/ 'I Should Have Known Better'.

1 APRIL
Lennon's father, Freddie, dies at Brighton General Hospital at the age of 63. During the final weeks of his life, John and Freddie have finally reached some kind of stability in their relationship, albeit via telephone on opposite sides of the Atlantic.

APRIL
John makes his last appearance in a professional recording studio for more than four years, when he helps Ringo record the inane 'Cookin' '.

Studio recording:
'Cookin' '.

31 MAY
Capitol Records issue their first Beatles single since 1968, when 'Got To Get You Into My Life' is used to première an upcoming compilation.

JUNE-JULY
While Yoko and Sean remain at the Dakota, Lennon spends several weeks at the family's Long Island home. While he's there, he tapes several readings from what becomes *Skywriting By Word Of Mouth*, the book he began writing the previous year. He also pens an introduction for *Rock'n'Roll Times*, a collection of photos by his old friend from Hamburg, Jurgen Vollmer.

Meanwhile, the Lennons reveal this summer that they intend to publish a book entitled *365 Days Of Sean*, comprising one photo of their son from each day of his first year of life. The book never appears.

7 JUNE
Capitol release a double-LP set of previously issued Beatles tracks, 'Rock 'N' Roll Music'.

Lennon's offer to design the sleeve is rejected; and he is appalled when he plays the album to hear that many of the songs have been remixed.

11 JUNE
'Rock 'N' Roll Music' is released in Britain.

25 JUNE
Maintaining the run of post-Beatles singles featuring McCartney, not Lennon, Parlophone release 'Back In The USSR'.

27 JULY
Lennon's victory in his immigration case is complete, when Judge Ira Fieldsteel grants him permanent residential status in the USA, and the right to apply for full citizenship in 1981. The court hearing is little more than a formality, but just to be sure, Lennon amasses a formidable array of celebrity witnesses, including Norman Mailer, Gloria Swanson and Geraldo Rivera. They testify to his stature as an artist and his commitment to international goodwill and justice. Quizzed by the Judge about his intentions, Lennon says that he intends to remain in America: "I hope to continue living here with my family and make music."

At one point during the proceedings the Judge inquires whether Lennon is 'likely to become a state charge', whereupon Leon Wildes assures the court that Lennon's assets are such this is most unlikely to occur.

Afterwards, a proud, short-haired, besuited Lennon poses for photographers with his 'green card' (No. A17-597-321). He is amused to discover that his 'green card' is actually blue. Once the celebrations are over, he retires to the seclusion of his Dakota apartment.

John Lennon: "I have a love for this country. If it were two thousand years ago, we'd all want to live in Rome. This is Rome now."

From this point onwards John ceases his regular communication with the music press. Responding to a request for an interview by his media

John with his 'green' card.

friend Chris Charlesworth, *Melody Maker*'s US Editor, he sends a postcard on which he writes: 'I am invisible'.

30 JULY
Polydor issue a double-LP of interviews with individual members of The Beatles, 'The Beatles Tapes'. It includes 20 minutes of conversation between the Lennons and journalist David Wigg conducted in June 1969, and a further nine minutes from October 1971. Attempts by The Beatles to block the release fail.

MID-AUGUST
Photographer Nishi Saimaru becomes the Lennons' in-house assistant. He accompanies them to visit a macrobiotics instructor in Boston.
    Around this time, Lennon – who subsequently pledges that he didn't touch his guitar between 1976 and 1980 – begins to record home demos of new songs like 'She Is A Friend Of Dorothy' and a revamped 'Tennessee'. He also returns to a 1970 composition, 'Sally And Billy', and for his own amusement records an acoustic take of the Jimmy Cliff classic, 'Many Rivers To Cross'.

8 NOVEMBER
Another McCartney-sung Beatles single is released in the States, 'Ob-La-Di, Ob-La-Da'.

19 NOVEMBER
Nine years late, the 'Magical Mystery Tour' LP by The Beatles is finally released in Britain.

1977

10 JANUARY
Allen Klein's legal battle with the ex-Beatles is settled, when he agrees to pay the group $800,000. In return, The Beatles have to pay Klein's ABKCO organisation many times that amount in unpaid management fees. Lennon and Ono appear alongside Klein for a publicity photograph to mark the agreement: both sides praise Ono's negotiating skills as the key to settling the complex legal situation.

MID-JANUARY
John and Yoko make a rare public appearance, at President Jimmy Carter's inaugural ball in Washington DC.

MARCH
Film director Francis Ford Coppola invites Lennon to contribute the soundtrack music for the movie that will become *Apocalypse Now*. Lennon declines to answer, let alone write the music.
    John, Yoko and Sean spend several days with artist George Maciunas at his Massachusetts farm, where they are photographed by their friend Nishi Saimaru.

APRIL
The Lennon family visit the circus at Madison Square Garden in New York, where they are joined by fellow spectator Mick Jagger, and interviewed by a TV crew covering the event.

4 APRIL
For no apparent reason, Capitol issue another US John Lennon single, 'Stand By Me'/'Woman Is The Nigger Of The World'.

8 APRIL
Legal attempts by The Beatles to prevent the release of a batch of tapes recorded live in Hamburg on December 31, 1962 fail, as the German label Bellaphon issue 'The Beatles Live! At The Star Club In Hamburg, Germany, 1962'. Although the sound quality is mediocre and some of the performances lacklustre, the double-LP introduces the world to the sound of The Beatles live on stage before their first major hit. The set captures some of Lennon's acerbic comments to the German audience, and some stunning lead vocals from him on tracks like 'Twist And Shout', 'Little Queenie' and 'Sweet Little Sixteen'. Intriguingly, though, McCartney performs twice as many numbers as Lennon.

MAY
Yoko has been acting on John's behalf in business meetings for the past year: now she is appointed his official representative.

4 MAY
One of the reasons for The Beatles' lack of enthusiasm for the release of the Hamburg tapes becomes clear when Capitol issue 'The Beatles At The Hollywood Bowl', a carefully assembled collage of songs from their 1964 and 1965 concerts at that venue. Most critics opt for the Star Club release when it comes to excitement.

6 MAY
UK release date for the 'Hollywood Bowl' LP.

25 MAY
'The Beatles Live! At The Star Club' is released in Britain.

EARLY JUNE
The Lennons migrate to Tokyo for a summer-long visit, spending three of their four months in the country staying in small hotels outside the capital. For much of the time, they are charged with looking after a collection of Yoko's young nieces. They also spend some time with her mother, who makes her disapproval of Lennon very apparent.
    The trip begins with a stopover in Hong Kong, where the family stay at the Mandarin Hotel. One night during their time there, they dine with David Bowie.

13 JUNE
'The Beatles Live! At The Star Club' appears in the States, with four different songs from the European releases. These include two additional Lennon vehicles, 'Where Have You Been All My Life' and 'I'm Gonna Sit Right Down And Cry'.

24 JUNE
Lennon finally wins the lead vocal on a post-1970 Beatles single. Sadly, it's an unofficial release of 'Twist And Shout', taken from the Star Club tapes.

JULY

After their stay in Tokyo, the Lennons move on to the resort of Karuizawa.

16 AUGUST

Elvis Presley dies in Memphis, Tennessee. Pressured for a public comment in Japan, Lennon issues a statement via Elliot Mintz in New York: "Elvis died when he went into the Army". Two days later, Mintz joins the Lennons in Japan.

LATE AUGUST

Thrilled by the monotony of his Japanese holiday, Lennon tells Tarot Card reader John Green, "I'm dead".

LATE SEPTEMBER

Staying at the Hotel Okura in Tokyo with Yoko, Sean and Elliot Mintz, Lennon inadvertently gives his last 'public' performance. He is singing 'Jealous Guy' to Mintz in his enormous Imperial Suite, when a Japanese couple enter the room by mistake, assuming it's the dining suite. They mistake Lennon for the night's entertainment, wait politely for service, and then leave in disgust when no-one arrives to take their order.

Around the same time, he records guitar demos of a new song, 'Mirror Mirror', which he tells Mintz is one of the numbers set aside for the autobiographical musical he is planning with his wife, *The Ballad Of John And Yoko*. John Green alleges that the musical was actually nothing more than a scheme by Yoko to keep Lennon busy, while she pursued her own interests.

4 OCTOBER

At the end of their four-month visit to Japan, the Lennons hold a press conference. Their first public appearance in more than a year, it passes almost unnoticed by Western media. Lennon announces that he will continue to concentrate on raising his child, and that he has no intentions of returning to active artistic life. It is reported that Lennon boasts "I have made my contribution to society" during this press conference, though he subsequently denies making this remark.

MID-OCTOBER

Lennon tapes piano demos of 'Mirror Mirror', at the Dakota.

He has returned home from Japan with a new portable mixing desk, which enables him to create a series of collage recordings he calls 'mind movies'. These mixes of comedy routines and found sounds are sent as aural postcards to friends like Elliot Mintz.

LATE OCTOBER

At a New York party for Rod Stewart, the Lennons run into May Pang; no words are exchanged in public, though Pang and Lennon are still meeting every few weeks.

21 OCTOBER

Another fatuous double-LP is concocted from The Beatles catalogue, as 'Love Songs' appears on Capitol. 'Girl' is briefly proposed as a tie-in single, but is cancelled in November.

NOVEMBER/DECEMBER

In a flurry of creative activity, Lennon writes and tapes demos of several new songs, including 'Real Life', 'Emotional Wreck', 'Whatever Happened To...', 'One Of The Boys', 'I Don't Wanna Face It', 'Free As A Bird' and 'I Watch Your Face'. Their overwhelming mood is one of depression and inadequacy.

11 NOVEMBER

Time for 'Love Songs' to flood UK stores.

EARLY DECEMBER

The Lennons purchase a herd of pedigree cows in Delaware County as a tax dodge.

LATE DECEMBER

John spends Christmas in Florida with his first son, Julian, who has travelled down with John and Yoko from New York.

He also ends his affair with May Pang by default, failing to contact her for almost a year.

1978

JANUARY

According to the testimony of John Green, Lennon retires to his Dakota bedroom this month, and "remained there for the next 15 months". His public activities during this period are certainly at an all-time low, as is his creativity. He spends his days watching TV, reading, smoking and sleeping. Yoko, meanwhile, is free to concentrate on her business affairs, and on assembling a sizeable collection of Egyptian art.

During this year, however, Lennon does write the prose essay included in the *Skywriting By Word Of Mouth* book under the title 'The Ballad Of John And Yoko'. It has been suggested that this provocative, collage-like piece was intended for the theatre programme when the musical of the same name opened, but it is unusual to pen the programme notes before the musical itself has been composed. The fragmented nature of the article suggests that it may have been pieced together from unfinished journal or diary entries after John's death.

Either way, it ends in uncompromising fashion: "I am blessed with a second chance. Being a Beatle nearly cost me my life, and certainly cost me a great deal of my health... all in an effort to reach 'out there'. I will not make the same mistake twice in one lifetime. This time around, inspiration will be called down by the ancient methods laid down for all to see. If I never 'produce' anything more for public consumption than 'silence', so be it. Amen."

MARCH

Lennon wastes his time and his imagination, recording a trio of supposedly humourous skits, based around the exploits of French detective Maurice Dupont. Elliot Mintz is amused.

JUNE

A private jet takes the Lennons to Grand Cayman Island in the Caribbean for a short vacation.

JULY

The Lennons make another visit to Japan: John apparently spends almost the entire vacation locked in his hotel room.

7 AUGUST

As the wretched *Sgt. Pepper's Lonely Hearts Club Band* movie flops around the world, Capitol attempt to cash in on The Bee Gees' perversion of The Beatles' original concept by issuing the opening medley of the 1967 album as a single.

22 SEPTEMBER

Britain receives the dubious pleasure of the 'Sgt. Pepper' single.

9 OCTOBER

Sean's third birthday is celebrated at the Lennons' favourite New York restaurant, the Tavern On The Green.

NOVEMBER/DECEMBER

Maybe it's the time of year... once again, Lennon greets the onset of a New York winter with a brief spout of creative writing, reworking the previous year's 'Emotional Wreck' as 'People', and beginning two new songs, 'Everybody's Talkin', Nobody's Talkin' and 'Stranger's Room'.

10 NOVEMBER

More Beatles repackaging, albeit with a bonus of sorts, as Parlophone unleash 'The Beatles Collection'. This 14-LP set reprises the entire official back catalogue by the band (not counting compilations), but adds a 'new' album entitled 'Rarities'. "This won't be available separately," claim EMI, with their fingers crossed behind their back.

DECEMBER

The Lennons quietly launch the Spirit Foundation, their own personal charity – with the Salvation Army the first beneficiaries.

1 DECEMBER

'The Beatles Collection' crosses the ocean to America, where 'Rarities' is stripped of two of its more interesting tracks. Old marketing habits die hard. John Lennon is sadly unavailable for comment.

EARLY DECEMBER
Lennon and May Pang meet and make love for the last time.

LATE DECEMBER
Lennon concocts a 'comic' sketch about the exploits of 'The Greak Wok', for the amusement of Elliot Mintz.

1979

JANUARY
The Lennons fly to Egypt to see the Pyramids, at the start of a period of intense travel that lasts into mid-February. Their precise movements during these weeks remain a mystery, though the couple are also believed to have spent some time in South Africa and Spain – as close as Lennon ever came to returning to Britain after September 1971.

The chronology of Lennon's travels in the late Seventies remains muddled, at best – not helped by the deliberate ambiguity of his comments in his 1980 interviews. He mentions then a solo visit to Hong Kong; Elliot Mintz elsewhere recounts a visit he and John made to Germany. Most evidence points towards

the South African visit as taking place early in 1979; but May Pang dates it as May 1980.

All this activity suggests a carefree, jet-setting lifestyle, but Lennon insiders tend to agree on one point: John only travelled where and when Yoko told him to, and her instructions were often inspired by Tarot Card readings.

19 FEBRUARY
Yoko Ono appoints Fred Seaman as John's personal assistant. Over the remaining 22 months of John's life, Seaman becomes his closest daily confidant outside the immediate family.

MARCH
The Lennon family decamps to Palm Beach, Florida, for a vacation, where they are joined by John's son Julian and three of Yoko's nieces.

Fred Seaman: "In the evenings, father and son sometimes sat down after dinner with two guitars, and John would begin teaching Julian new chords, passing on a little bit of the legacy hand to hand. Most of the time, John showed no effort to make any meaningful contact with Julian. They always seemed like separate people in separate dreams."

11 MAY
The repackaging industry continues apace, as the US 'Hey Jude' LP from 1970 is finally released in Britain.

27 MAY
A full-page advertisement runs in newspapers in London, New York and Tokyo, under the title: 'A Love Letter From John And Yoko To People Who Ask Us What, When And Why'. It bears all the hallmarks of Ono's prose, not Lennon's, but its message of carefree, naïve idealism and pleasure in placidity suggests that the couple are enjoying an idyllic family life – despite the subsequent testimony of ex-friends and 'insiders'.

JUNE
John, Yoko and Sean leave New York for Japan, where they remain for the summer until the start of September.

5 SEPTEMBER
Over the next few months, Lennon tape-records his memoirs, which develop into an acerbic assault on many of the important figures from his past, including members of his family and the other ex-Beatles.

OCTOBER
Former Beatles promoter Sid Bernstein makes one of his regular appeals for the group to re-form for a charity concert – this time to raise funds for the Vietnamese boat people. Lennon is the only one of the four to respond positively, but after sending more information to the Dakota, as requested, Bernstein hears no more from him.

United Nations secretary-general Kurt Waldheim is engaged on a similar mission, and he also contacts The Beatles. This time, Yoko refuses to respond officially, though the offer obviously attracts Lennon, who writes to a friend: "Looks like the boys and I will be playing for those sailing enthusiasts, the Boat People."

He doesn't, and McCartney takes on the burden of saving the boat people without him; but Lennon does begin another of his annual bouts of songwriting. Between now and the end of the year, he begins to compose a song for Sean, 'Beautiful Boy', revamps 'Real Life' from 1977 as 'Real Love', and lays the foundations for two of the 'Double Fantasy' songs – 'Starting Over' (known at this point as 'My Life') and 'Watching The Wheels' (alias 'I'm Crazy').

107

9 OCTOBER
John and Yoko hire Le Roy's Tavern On The Green, an exclusive New York restaurant in Central Park, for Sean's fourth birthday party. Lennon spends the next three weeks inside the Dakota, cut off from the outside world.

15 OCTOBER
The Lennons contribute $1,000 to the Patrolmen's Benevolent Association, a New York fund to provide bulletproof vests for the city's police officers – a far cry from the anti-police rhetoric of early Seventies songs like 'Attica State' and 'John Sinclair'.

19 OCTOBER
Eleven months after promising that The Beatles' 'Rarities' album will be available only in the expensive box set 'The Beatles Collection', EMI release it on its own.

31 OCTOBER
Lennon briefly leaves the seclusion of the Dakota to experience the real world, taking Sean to see *Peter Pan* on Broadway.

LATE NOVEMBER
The Lennons buy Cannon Hill, a mansion on Cold Spring Harbor, Long Island. Fred Seaman: "John talked about the pleasures of having a country house where he could occasionally take LSD and psychedelic mushrooms in peace and quiet."

12 NOVEMBER
John Lennon signs his last will and testament, leaving the bulk of his estate to Yoko Ono.

LATE DECEMBER
Christmas is celebrated at the Lennons' Palm Beach estate.

31 DECEMBER
Many of the Lennons' joint companies, including Bag Productions, are officially dissolved on this date.
Lennon celebrates the New Year by staging the one and only meeting of the Club Dakota with Elliot Mintz. Dressed in black tie and tails, they invite their guests to partake of an evening of polite entertainment.

In the event, only one guest receives an invitation: Yoko Ono.

1980

JANUARY
From the testimony of Fred Seaman: "Yoko's behaviour became increasingly weird and was accompanied by a marked deterioration in her physical appearance. Her face was haggard, her eyes glassy around pinned pupils, and she began to spend much of her time in the bathroom making loud snorting noises, frequently followed by frightful retching. I realised she was strung out on heroin.
"On the rare occasions John met Yoko, they circled each other wearily. John would harangue Yoko about her vampire hours and her dishevelled, zombie-like appearance."

13 JANUARY
Another 'new' Beatles LP hits US stores, as 'Hear The Beatles Tell All', an interview album previously available only to DJs back in 1964, is released.

14 JANUARY
Paul McCartney, staying in New York, phones Lennon and suggests a meeting, so they can share "some dynamite weed". Lennon freaks out when he hears that McCartney is headed for Japan – and his favourite Tokyo hotel suite.

16 JANUARY
Paul McCartney is arrested on drugs charges as he enters Japan for a Wings tour. Some commentators on Lennon's career have gone so far as to allege that Yoko Ono was able to manoeuvre the arrest from long distance.
Fred Seaman: "John firmly believed that Yoko had managed to cast a spell on Paul."

FEBRUARY
Lennon and Ono holiday in Palm Beach, with actor Peter Boyle and his wife Loraine Alterman. John returns to New York revitalised, telling friends that

he is ready for a period of "constant rebirth".
To prove the point, he returns to several of the songs he's started in recent years. 'My Life' from 1979 becomes 'Don't Be Crazy' and then 'The Worst Is Over', en route to 'Starting Over'. 'Beautiful Boy' and 'Watching The Wheels' are virtually completed, while Lennon also writes songs called 'Across The River' and 'Memories' around similar chords. He comes close to finishing another new song, 'Clean-Up Time', and reworks the 'Real Love' theme one more time, titling this effort 'Girls And Boys'.
The most powerful song from these writing sessions, however, remains unreleased. 'Serve Yourself' is a direct response to Bob Dylan's sly piece of evangelical fervour, 'Gotta Serve Somebody', in which he nailed his colours to a Christian cross. Lennon's reply is bitter and sarcastic, and continues the sceptical tradition of 1970's 'God'. He cuts around a dozen bluesy piano demos of the song, to which he will return that summer.

20 MARCH
John and Yoko celebrate their 11th wedding anniversary in lavish style. She buys him a celebratory Rolls-Royce; he responds with 500 gardenias and a heart-shaped diamond.

24 MARCH
Capitol in the States revamps the 'Rarities' LP from 'The Beatles Collection' box set, and issues it as a separate item.

9 APRIL
Yoko, John and Sean travel to their Long Island house for another vacation.

19 APRIL
Lennon begins a ten-day "vow of silence" at Yoko's suggestion, to "clean out his head".

30 APRIL
Lennon ends his period of silence by ritually shaving off his beard, for the first time since the previous summer.

LATE MAY
According to May Pang, Lennon phones her from South Africa at this time, and sends her a postcard from Cape Town. This trip isn't mentioned in other insider accounts of Lennon's final year, but Pang's book does illustrate the postcard as evidence. Other sources confirm that John was booked at the Mount Nelson Hotel in Cape Town around this time, apparently under the name of the Lennons' Tarot Card reader, John Green.

2 JUNE
At an auction in Syracuse, New York, dairy farmer Steve Potter pays $265,000 for a single Holstein cow owned by the Lennons.

4 JUNE
Lennon and several friends sail from Newport, Rhode Island to Bermuda. En route, their boat hits a major storm, during which John is the only crew member fit enough to take the helm. He excitedly tells friends that the experience has left him more "centred" in himself than he has been in more than a decade.

12 JUNE
Lennon's voyage on the yacht *Megan Jaye* comes to an end.

16 JUNE
Sean Lennon and Fred Seaman join Lennon in Bermuda.

21 JUNE
Inspired by listening to Bob Marley's 'Burnin'' album, Lennon composes 'Borrowed Time'.

22 JUNE
Lennon cuts double-tracked acoustic demos of 'Watching The Wheels', a song which he's been working on slowly for several years, and 'I Don't Want To Face It' and 'Borrowed Time', both written in Bermuda. That night, Seaman accompanies Lennon on a trip to the local nightclub, Flavors, where Lennon hears the B-52s' 'Rock Lobster' for the first time, and remarks on its similarity to Yoko's work from the early Seventies.

23 JUNE
The previous night's activities spark another new song from Lennon, 'I'm Steppin' Out'.

24 JUNE
In the Bermuda Botanical Gardens, Lennon spots a freesia hybrid named *Double Fantasy*. He borrows the title for the album he is already envisaging for when he returns to New York.

25 JUNE
Lennon invests in a more expensive home-recording machine, and begins to tape demos of songs like 'Serve Yourself', 'Beautiful Boy' and 'Watching The Wheels'.

27 JUNE
Yoko arrives in Bermuda; Lennon performs the bulk of his new material, including an expletive-filled take of 'Serve Yourself', in an effort to win her approval. It's seething with anger and sarcasm, and heavy with undeleted expletives; and for sheer savagery, it tops even 'How Do You Sleep'.

29 JUNE
To Lennon's disgust, Yoko returns to New York – alone.

1 JULY
Unable to reach Yoko on the phone, Lennon composes the song 'I'm Losing You'. He also records 'Dear Yoko' for the first time.

4 JULY
Fred Seaman returns to New York, and hears rumours from some of Yoko's circle that she plans to divorce John.

18 JULY
While Lennon sits for a portrait in Bermuda, intended as a present for Yoko, she is spending the weekend with her close friend, art dealer Sam Green.

MID-TO-LATE JULY
Yoko begins playing her new songs down the phone to John, from New York to Bermuda. Gradually, the concept of 'Double Fantasy' as a conversation through music takes shape. Lennon begins to talk about a schedule for the next few months that will see their album released in the autumn, and then the couple collaborating on a Broadway show. During this period, he also writes the final song of his Bermuda vacation, 'Woman', and begins work on a cod country tune, 'Life Begins At 40'.

29 JULY
John and Sean fly back to New York, where (according to Fred Seaman) "Yoko had abandoned her plan to divorce John".

> "I am blessed with a second chance. Being a Beatle nearly cost me my life, and certainly cost me a great deal of my health... all in an effort to reach 'out there'. I will not make the same mistake twice in one lifetime. This time around, inspiration will be called down by the ancient methods laid down for all to see. If I never 'produce' anything more for public consumption than 'silence', so be it. Amen."

31 JULY
The Lennons arrange a meeting with record producer Jack Douglas, to discuss working with him on their forthcoming project. Douglas, who acted as engineer on some of John and Yoko's early Seventies projects, initially refuses to take the job unless he is the sole producer, but eventually agrees to share the role with his clients.

1 AUGUST
Jack Douglas immediately books the Hit Factory studios for the Lennons to begin recording, but is stalled by Lennon, who feels that Yoko's songs are not yet sufficiently complete. Meanwhile, John works on the lyrics of a new song, 'Forgive Me, My Little Flower Princess', apparently written for May Pang.

2 AUGUST
The Lennons stage a rehearsal with musicians Hugh McCracken, George Small and Tony Davilio at the Dakota, supervised by Jack Douglas. Among the songs they attempt are 'Beautiful Boy', 'I'm Your Angel' and 'Borrowed Time'.

3 AUGUST
John and Yoko spend the next two days at Sam Green's house on Fire island.

4 AUGUST
The Lennons return to the Dakota in time for an evening rehearsal, during which they perform 'Kiss Kiss Kiss', 'Every Man Has A Woman Who Loves Him' and 'I'm Moving On'.

7 AUGUST
Recording sessions for what becomes 'Double Fantasy' begin at the Hit Factory in New York. Initially, the Lennons use musicians Earl Slick, Tony Levin, Arthur Jenkins and Andy Newmark, not the men with whom they have just been rehearsing. During the day's work, Lennon continually flirts with a guitar riff that turns into his unreleased song, 'Gone From This Place'.
Studio recordings:
'I'm Stepping Out', 'Borrowed Time'.

8 AUGUST
Lennon smokes pot ostentatiously as the band continue the sessions.
Studio recordings:
'Nobody Told Me', 'Kiss Kiss Kiss'.

9 AUGUST
As Yoko fluffs her vocals one time too often, Lennon lets rip: "Remember the bridge on the River Kwai, you fuck!".
Studio recording:
'Don't Be Scared'.

12 AUGUST
Lennon and Ono issue a press release announcing their comeback, and noting that one of the themes of their album is the "exploration of sexual fantasies between men and women".

For the second week of sessions, Bun E. Carlos and Rick Nielsen of Cheap Trick are invited to take part, though their contribution is restricted to one song. Thereafter, the previous week's line-up takes over.
Studio recordings:
'I'm Losing You', 'Beautiful Boy'.

13 AUGUST
George Harrison rings the Dakota and suggests collaborating with John; John ignores the message, still bitter over Harrison's decision to scarcely mention him in his recently published autobiography, *I Me Mine*.
Studio recording:
'Cleanup Time'.

14 AUGUST
Yoko misses the day's session, in favour of spending time with her friend Sam Green.
Studio recording:
'Forgive Me, My Little Flower Princess'.

but when Yoko says exactly the same thing, he quips: "An ex-Beatle, you fucking cunt. In fact, I'm supposed to sound like Smokey Robinson, my dear."

Studio recording:
'Woman', 'Beautiful Boy', 'I Don't Wanna Face It', 'Watching The Wheels', 'Dear Yoko', 'Every Man Has A Woman Who Loves Him', 'Real Love', '(Just Like) Starting Over'.

24 AUGUST
Sean Lennon is in the Hit Factory for this session, to see his father overdubbing guitar parts on '(Just Like) Starting Over'.

5 SEPTEMBER
Horn overdubs are recorded for the 'Double Fantasy' songs.

9 SEPTEMBER
Playboy reporter David Sheff begins three weeks in the Lennons' company, gathering material for a lengthy interview to be published in the magazine's January 1981 edition, and in extended book-length

form in December 1981. Besides covering the remaining recording sessions, and receiving the full benefit of the John and Yoko myth of eternal happiness and creativity, Sheff guides Lennon through a song-by-song analysis of his Beatles and solo catalogue.

10 SEPTEMBER
A black teenage girl choir adds its collective voice to one of Yoko's songs, and also records a chant of "One world, one people", which is intended as the climax of the album.

Studio recording:
'Hard Times Are Over'.

19 SEPTEMBER
Yoko Ono meets David Geffen, having consulted his astrological numbers beforehand to discover whether it's worth seeing him. He agrees a deal to release the 'Double Fantasy' album, without having heard a note of what they've recorded.

15 AUGUST
Studio recording:
'Beautiful Boys'.

18 AUGUST
Yoko recruits a video crew to film the evening's recording session. Caught on tape are impromptu versions of several rock oldies, plus attempts by the band to drag Lennon into performing some vintage Beatles songs. The resulting footage is intended for the 'Starting Over' promo video.

19 AUGUST
Studio recording:
'Hard Times Are Over'.

20 AUGUST – 3 SEPTEMBER
The Hit Factory sessions continue, producing an average of around one song per day.

The highlight of these sessions is 'Woman', which Lennon introduces to the band as "early Motown/Beatles, *circa* 64. It's for your mother or your sister, anyone of the female race. That's who you're singing to." "I feel like I'm in the fucking Beatles with that track," he remarks during the sessions,

22 SEPTEMBER
Lennon, Ono and Geffen sign the fateful recording contract.

24 SEPTEMBER
Sessions move from the Hit Factory to the Record Plant East, where Douglas is ready to begin the final mixing.

25 SEPTEMBER
Yoko has a meeting with Sean's bodyguard, Doug MacDougall, to discuss increasing the security around the Lennons, in response to the number of fans who are now camping out by the Dakota in the hope of seeing John leaving for another session. They agree to differ over the solution to the problem, and schedule another meeting for December 9.

26 SEPTEMBER
Jack Douglas prepares the single mixes of '(Just Like) Starting Over' and 'Kiss Kiss Kiss'. The sound of a Japanese wishing bell is added to the beginning of Lennon's song, as a deliberate echo of the funereal bells which opened 'Mother' on John's 1970 LP.

29 SEPTEMBER
Newsweek magazine lands the scoop of publishing the first interview from the Lennons' comeback. In Honolulu, longtime Beatles fan Mark Chapman reads Barbara Graustark's story, and is convinced that Lennon is "a phony". Playing old Beatles and Lennon albums demonstrates to Chapman the extent of the star's hypocrisy.

Though he has no way of knowing this, the accusation of phoniness is at least partially correct. Beginning with the *Newsweek* interview, and continuing right up to his death, Lennon misleads the media into believing that he has made no attempt at songwriting between 1975 and summer 1980, and that all the 'Double Fantasy' songs emerged intact during his time in Bermuda. Only after his death, when dozens of late Seventies acoustic demos are discovered among his effects, is this proved to have been at best a PR line.

Meanwhile, sound effects, taped in the streets of New York by engineer Jon Smith and the Lennons' assistant, Fred Seaman, are added to 'Watching The Wheels' and 'I'm Your Angel'.

30 SEPTEMBER
Mixing sessions are halted when Yoko Ono insists that the entire company move back to the Hit Factory.

3 OCTOBER
The Beatles industry plumbs new depths, as Parlophone prepare 'The Beatles Ballads', almost half of which also appeared on 'Love Songs'.

9 OCTOBER
Lennon's 40th birthday is marked by a gathering of fans outside the Dakota Building. Lennon sleeps through the festivities, while a plane hired by Yoko writes the message 'Happy Birthday John + Sean – Love Yoko' nine times in the sky. Spokesman Fred Seaman confirms that the couple will be touring Japan, Europe and the USA in the spring.

John and Yoko simulating sex for
the cameras, in a clip used in the
'Walking On Thin Ice' video.

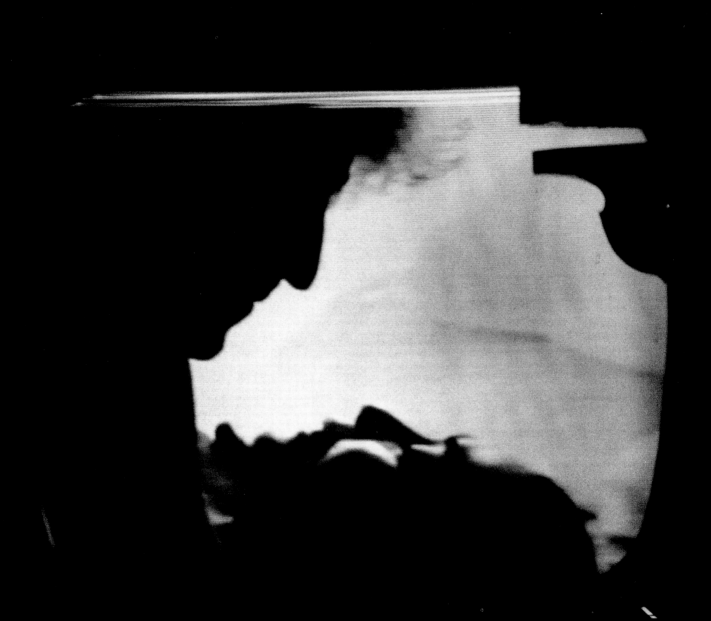

12 OCTOBER
John and Sean share a belated birthday party at the Tavern On The Green.

17 OCTOBER
The first new single of John Lennon music in more than five years is released by Geffen in the States. '(Just Like) Starting Over' finds Lennon in unexpectedly lighthearted mood, pasticing the vocal mannerisms of Fifties rockers. The combination of humour and sentimentality disarms and confuses many listeners, who have been expecting the return of the politicised, heavily ironic Lennon of old. The flipside, Yoko's orgasmic 'Kiss Kiss Kiss', conforms more to expectations.

18 OCTOBER
Mark Chapman borrows Anthony Fawcett's book, *John Lennon: One Day At A Time*, from Honolulu Public Library. In the book he finds evidence – at least, to his own satisfaction – that Lennon is a hypocrite who has sold out all his original ideals and principles. Chapman, who has been psychologically disturbed for more than a decade, decides over the next few weeks that the 'solution' to his mental turmoil is to kill John Lennon.

20 OCTOBER
'Double Fantasy' is finally mixed and mastered to the Lennons' joint satisfaction.

23 OCTOBER
Mark Chapman signs off from his job as a Honolulu maintenance man, using the pseudonym 'John Lennon'.

24 OCTOBER
'(Just Like) Starting Over' is released in Britain, to generally unappreciative reviews.

29 OCTOBER
Mark Chapman flies from Honolulu to New York, carrying with him a handgun, but no ammunition.

30 OCTOBER
Chapman visits the Dakota for the first time, returning every morning for the next five days. He tries to buy ammunition, but fails.

NOVEMBER
With one album ready for release, and the raw material assembled for another, Lennon keeps writing: this month, he tapes home demos of the elegiac 'Grow Old With Me', and the work-in-progress 'Gone From This Place'.

3 NOVEMBER
Coinciding neatly with Lennon's reappearance, EMI's UK mail order division issue 'The Beatles Box', an eight-LP set which includes a selection of much-hyped, but unexceptional, 'rarities'.

5 NOVEMBER
Frustrated by his inability to buy bullets in New York, Mark Chapman flies to Atlanta, Georgia, to visit an old friend.

9 NOVEMBER
Chapman returns to New York; on the plane, he reads an *Esquire* article by Laurence Shames, which sarcastically counterposes John Lennon's radical beliefs and exclusive lifestyle. On arrival, he returns to his Dakota vigil, though he is repeatedly told that the Lennons are out of town for the week.

11 NOVEMBER
Chapman phones his wife in Hawaii and admits that he has been planning to murder John Lennon. She persuades him to return home the next day.

14 NOVEMBER
'Double Fantasy' by John Lennon and Yoko Ono signals a full-blooded return to the limelight, even if the artistic renaissance isn't quite as certain. It has two songs equal to Lennon's best work, 'Woman' and 'Watching The Wheels', but his remaining five compositions sound more like pastiches than fully-fledged evidence of genius. Yoko's material, meanwhile, successfully updates the sound of her early Seventies records in keeping with the prevailing currents of new wave and disco.

17 NOVEMBER
UK release date for 'Double Fantasy'. Most British rock critics praise Yoko at Lennon's expense, but slam the record as a whole.
 Melody Maker: "The whole thing positively reeks of an indulgent sterility... it's a godawful yawn."
 New Musical Express: "The album is self-centred to the point of utter solipsism... it's a lousy record."

25 NOVEMBER
'Double Fantasy' enters the US album chart at No. 25. The Lennons celebrate with light lunch at Café La Fortuna, then head back to the Hit Factory for another session.

26 NOVEMBER
Yoko organises a video shoot at the Sperone Gallery in Soho, during which the Lennons pose in the nude and simulate sex for the cameras.

28 NOVEMBER
As part of a legal battle by the ex-Beatles to halt a stage show called *Beatlemania*, Lennon signs an affidavit to the effect that the four Beatles have agreed to take part in a reunion concert at some stage in the early Eighties. The reunion would provide the finale to *The Long And Winding Road*, Apple's official documentary film history of The Beatles' career.

EARLY DECEMBER

John and Yoko agree to lend their support to a demonstration planned for San Francisco, in support of Japanese workers employed by local food importers who are on strike for better wages.

The Lennons issue a statement: "We are with you in spirit. Both of us are subjected to prejudice and abuse as an Oriental family in the Western world. Boycott it must be, if it is the only way to bring justice and restore the dignity of the constitution for the sake of all citizens of the US and their children. Peace and love, John Lennon and Yoko Ono, New York City, December 1980."

The couple agree to join a protest march planned for the second week of the month, and book their plane tickets to San Francisco.

1-5 DECEMBER

The Lennons mix promotional duties with recording sessions for Yoko's new song, 'Walking On Thin Ice', which is being planned as her next single.

At home, meanwhile, Lennon tapes composing demos of two unfinished songs. 'Dear John' is a gentle piece of self-encouragement, but 'You Saved My Soul' is a remarkable confessional song, in which Lennon reveals that he'd once threatened to commit suicide by throwing himself from a Dakota window, and that only Yoko's intervention had saved him. Sadly, none of his final interviewees has heard the song, or is able to ask him about this incident – which is utterly at odds with the message he's feeding the press, that's he's spent five years since 1975 as a happy, secure house-husband and father.

2 DECEMBER

Mark Chapman boards a plane in Honolulu, en route to Chicago.

3 DECEMBER

SoHo News, a local New York paper, appears with a cover story on Yoko, under the banner headline: "Yoko Only".

Annie Leibovitz photographs

Lennon at the Dakota for *Rolling Stone* magazine.

5 DECEMBER

John and Yoko interviewed by Jonathan Cott for *Rolling Stone*. Cott questions some of the more exotic claims in Lennon's publicity story, and is greeted with a sometimes vitriolic response.

The interview continues at the Record Plant, where Lennon is remixing 'Every Man Has A Woman Who Loves Him', 'Open Your Box', 'Kiss Kiss Kiss' and 'Walking On Thin Ice' for release as a Yoko Ono EP.

Mark Chapman arrives in New York, after three days at his grandmother's home in Chicago.

6 DECEMBER

BBC DJ Andy Peebles interviews the Lennons for Radio One, at the Record Plant studio. Unlike Cott the previous day, he finds Lennon in good-humoured, nostalgic mood, ready for a gentle, non-confrontational stroll through his last 11 years. The text of this interview is published in book form as *The Lennon Tapes* in February 1981.

Mark Chapman checks into the YMCA on 63rd Street, and then walks to the Dakota, in the hope of seeing John Lennon. He also buys a copy of 'Double Fantasy'. He leaves the Dakota shortly before the Lennons return home from their BBC interview.

7 DECEMBER

Mark Chapman moves to the expensive Sheraton Hotel – from where he mounts another trip to the Dakota. During the day, he buys a copy of the January issue of *Playboy* magazine, with its lengthy Lennon interview. Back in his hotel room, he entertains a prostitute, and then adds the word 'Lennon' to the title of 'The Gospel According To John' in the room's copy of the Bible.

8 DECEMBER

American Eastern Time:

7.30am: Lennon leaves the Dakota to take breakfast in a downtown restaurant.

8.00am: Mark Chapman leaves the Sheraton Hotel, carefully arranging his belongings – including his passport and his defaced edition of the Bible – in his room before he departs.

10.00am: Chapman again walks to the Dakota, and begins to engage the security guard in casual conversation. He walks into Central Park, returning just in time to miss Lennon.

11.00am: *Rolling Stone* photographer Annie Leibovitz shoots a second session with the Lennons, including one shot which poses a naked John in a foetal position alongside a fully-clothed Yoko. "That's the cover," says John excitedly when he sees the Polaroid. "That's our relationship." The photo subsequently becomes the cover of the magazine's Lennon tribute issue early in 1981.

12.00 midday: Photographer

Paul Goresh has an uneasy discussion with Chapman, who is clutching his copy of 'Double Fantasy', outside the Dakota.

2.00pm: Inside the Dakota, the Lennons begin a three-hour interview with four journalists from RKO Radio of New York. Outside, a regular Lennon-watcher introduces Chapman to Sean Lennon and his nanny.

The RKO interview captures neither the relaxed Lennon of December 6, nor the combative interviewee of the day before that. Instead, Lennon races through lengthy analyses of his spiritual progress like a speed-freak, repeating again and again his faith in a life beyond death.

5.00pm: The Lennons emerge from the Dakota, and travel with the radio crew to the Record Plant East. Before leaving the Dakota, John signs a copy of 'Double Fantasy' for a fan, Mark Chapman from Hawaii, and is photographed in the act by Paul Goresh. Chapman remains open-mouthed and silent throughout the encounter, as if stunned by the presence of the ex-Beatle. "Is that all you want?" Lennon asks him. "Thanks, John," is all Chapman can reply.

5.30pm: Remixing continues on Yoko's 'Walking On Thin Ice', before the Lennons sift through a pile of mid-Seventies tapes recorded by Yoko with David Spinozza, in search of a potential B-side for her single.

8.00pm: Paul Goresh abandons his Dakota vigil, despite the entreaties of Mark Chapman that he remain. "What if you

never see him again?" Chapman asks. "What if something happens to him?"

10.30pm: John and Yoko complete work on 'Walking On Thin Ice' and leave the studio, telling the engineers that they are going out to eat at Stage Deli. Instead, they drive towards the Dakota.

10.50pm: The Lennons return by car from the studio to the Dakota, where they walk from the sidewalk to the building's entrance. Waiting in the shadows is Mark Chapman, who calls out: "Mr Lennon." John starts to turn towards him, and is greeted with a flurry of gunshots, striking him in the back and shoulders. He manages to stagger to the Dakota security guard's office, where he collapses, crying "I'm shot, I'm shot." Police are summoned to the Dakota, and Lennon – bleeding profusely, and his eyes reeling – is carried into a patrol vehicle. "Do you know who you are?" an officer asks him. Lennon attempts to answer, but is unable to force any words from his shattered vocal cords, before passing into unconsciousness.

Mark Chapman: "John Lennon got out of the limousine. He had something in his hands. Some cassette tapes. Nobody said a word. There was dead silence in my brain and John Lennon walked past me. He started walking faster as he went under the archway. Yoko was a little ahead of him. The voice said, 'Do it! Do it! Do it!'. "I aimed at his back. I pulled the trigger five times. The explosions were deafening. After the first shot, Yoko crouched down and ran around the corner, into the courtyard. Then the gun was empty and John Lennon had disappeared. Inside the Dakota, behind the door, some people were yelling. Somebody screamed. The doorman, Jose, was standing in front of me with tears in his eyes. 'Do you know what you've done?' he asked me."

Yoko Ono (from the notes of her official police interview after the shooting): "Went to Record Plant. Stayed until about 10.30. We wanted to go to restaurant but did not. We came back. We normally go into the gate but did not. Got out, walked past gate. John was walking past the door, he was walking faster. I heard shots. I heard shots. He walked to door upstairs. Said 'I'm shot'. I followed him. He was standing but staggering. I told him to lie down. Sometimes he was ahead, sometimes I was. I saw a male by the watchman's box. It was dark and night. He nodded at me – dark grayish clothing. Male, white. He was not small."

10.52pm: While Lennon is transported to Roosevelt Hospital, Chapman is arrested without a struggle. He is clutching a copy of J.D. Salinger's novel, *The Catcher In The Rye.*

11.00pm: Lennon arrives at Roosevelt Hospital, where frantic efforts are made to save his life. The damage caused by Chapman's hollow-point bullets is too severe, however, and John Lennon is officially pronounced dead at 11.15pm. Yoko, who has followed her husband to the hospital, is informed of John's death: "Do you mean that he is sleeping?" she responds hysterically.

9 DECEMBER
England wakes up the news that John Lennon has been shot. Radio stations play his and The Beatles' music constantly

> **Mark Chapman: "The voice said, 'Do it! Do it! Do it!'. I aimed at his back. I pulled the trigger five times. The explosions were deafening. After the first shot, Yoko crouched down and ran around the corner, into the courtyard. Then the gun was empty and John Lennon had disappeared. Inside the Dakota, behind the door, some people were yelling. Somebody screamed. The doorman, Jose, was standing in front of me with tears in his eyes. 'Do you know what you've done?' he asked me."**

throughout the day; newspapers are filled with the tragic news; old friends call each other up to share their grief; the nation mourns.

American Eastern time:
00.30am: Yoko Ono and David Geffen return to the Dakota. Yoko asks Lenono Music office manager Rich De Palma to break the news to John's Aunt Mimi, to his son Julian, and to Paul McCartney. Several thousand people are already gathered outside the Dakota, singing Lennon's songs.

1.05am: Mark Chapman signs a statement at 20th Precinct Police headquarters, admitting that he shot Lennon: "I can't believe I could do that," he tells officers. After speaking on the phone to his wife in Hawaii, he is moved to Bellevue Hospital, where psychiatric examination begins.

3.00am: Elliot Mintz arrives to supervise the chaotic scene inside the Dakota, and to comfort Yoko. She quickly tells him that she has decided that John should be cremated at a Hartsdale mortuary. Then she watches TV coverage of the murder.

3.30am: David Geffen talks to Yoko, and she dictates a statement asking fans to donate money in John's memory to the charity started by the Lennons, The Spirit Foundation. The funds received are subsequently

117

distributed to anti-war groups, New York health care programmes, and campaigns to combat child abuse, among others.

6.00am: The Dakota's main office receives a call from a Californian who says he is flying to New York "to finish the job Chapman started." The caller is intercepted by police at Los Angeles Airport, where he apparently says: "I'm gonna get Yoko Ono."

7.00am: Sean Lennon wakes up: for another 24 hours, no-one tells him what has happened.

Yoko returns upstairs to write a public announcement calling for John to be remembered with a silent vigil:

"There is no funeral for John. Later in the week we will set the time for a silent vigil to pray for his soul. We invite you to participate from wherever you

are at the time. We thank you for the many flowers sent to John. But in the future, instead of flowers, please consider sending donations in his name to the Spirit Foundation Inc., which is John's personal charitable foundation. He would have appreciated it very much. John loved and prayed for the human race. Please pray the same for him. Love, Yoko & Sean."

10.30am: An autopsy is carried out on John Lennon's body.

11.00am: Yoko receives word that a grief-stricken Lennon fan has committed suicide. She phones a message to the New York press, begging John's fans not to turn their anguish against themselves. Ringo Starr arrives in New York with his girlfriend, Barbara Bach. They are driven to the Dakota, and spend two hours with Yoko.

3.00pm: Mark Chapman is arraigned at the Manhattan Court House. On his lawyer's advice, he says nothing.

9.30pm: Julian Lennon flies into New York airport to be with Yoko and Sean. By the time he arrives at the Dakota, Yoko is – according to at least one 'insider' account – in a plush Harlem restaurant with David Geffen and Calvin Klein.

10 DECEMBER
American Eastern time:

7.00am: When Sean awakes, Yoko tells him that his father has been killed, and shows him where the murder took place. Sean asks why his father was shot. Yoko can say nothing.

2.00pm: John Lennon is cremated at Ferncliff Mortuary. It later transpires that the cremation was filmed, and that a mortuary assistant shot secret photos of Lennon's body on the

slab. These are sold to the press for $10,000.

9.00pm: Doug MacDougall returns from the crematorium with Lennon's ashes, and gives them to Yoko. Their subsequent fate is unconfirmed, though some reports suggest that they were secretly interred in Britain.

11 DECEMBER

Lennon's assistant, Fred Seaman, asks to be temporarily relieved of his duties at the Dakota.

Fred Seaman: "I woke up feeling lost, helpless and overwhelmed by a growing sense of dread. I could see that far from being the grief stricken widow she played for the media and for the detectives investigating John's murder, Yoko was determined to take advantage of this once-in-a-lifetime opportunity to forge a more positive public image and

Gunned down
by 'scre
as Yoko
on in h

force

LENONO
STUDIO ONE
1 WEST 72ND STREET
NEW YORK, NEW YORK 10023

I TOLD SEAN WHAT HAPPENED. I SHOWED HIM THE PICTURE OF HIS FATHER
ON THE COVER OF THE PAPER AND EXPLAINED THE SITUATION. I TOOK SEAN
TO THE SPOT WHERE JOHN LAY AFTER HE WAS SHOT. SEAN WANTED TO KNOW
WHY THE PERSON SHOT JOHN IF HE LIKED JOHN. I EXPLAINED THAT HE WAS
PROBABLY A CONFUSED PERSON. SEAN SAID WE SHOULD FIND OUT IF HE WAS
CONFUSED OR IF HE REALLY HAD MEANT TO KILL JOHN. I SAID THAT WAS UP
TO THE COURT. HE ASKED WHAT COURT - A TENNIS COURT OR A BASKETBALL
COURT? THAT'S HOW SEAN USED TO TALK WITH HIS FATHER. THEY WERE BUDDIES.
JOHN WOULD HAVE BEEN PROUD OF SEAN IF HE HAD HEARD THIS. SEAN CRIED
LATER. HE ALSO SAID "NOW DADDY IS PART OF GOD. I GUESS WHEN YOU DIE
YOU BECOME MUCH MORE BIGGER BECAUSE YOU'RE PART OF EVERYTHING"

I DON'T HAVE MUCH MORE TO ADD TO SEAN'S STATEMENT. THE SILENT VIGIL
WILL TAKE PLACE DECEMBER 14TH AT 2 P.M. FOR TEN MINUTES.

OUR THOUGHTS WILL BE WITH YOU.

                            Love,

                            Yoko & Sean
                            Dec. 10 '80
                            N.Y.C.

make money. Not wanting to be part of this campaign, I called Yoko and told her that I could no longer work for her."

Other sources suggest that Seaman is himself keen to capitalise on his insider information, and put together a book deal. Either way, he accompanies Julian to the Lennons' estate at Cold Spring Harbor for a short vacation.

12 DECEMBER
Yoko and producer Jack Douglas return to the Record Plant in New York for an exercise in emotional exorcism. "We went back into the studio and put together some collages with John's voice and music", Douglas explains. "It was almost like a funeral service. We teetered back and forth between hysteria and concentration. We did that for two nights. That seemed to provide some kind of therapy or release."

14 DECEMBER
At 2.00pm Eastern Standard Time (7.00pm in Britain), a worldwide 10-minute vigil of silence is observed in John Lennon's memory. The vigil is marked by commemorations in New York's Central Park and in Liverpool, both of which are broadcast live around the globe. Radio stations broadcast ten minutes of blank air as their contribution to the tribute. Yoko releases a statement after the event: "Bless you for your tears and prayers. I saw John smiling in the sky. I saw sorrow changing into clarity. I saw all of us becoming one mind. Thank you, Love, Yoko."

23 DECEMBER
Both 'Double Fantasy' and '(Just Like) Starting Over' reach the top of the US charts.

24 DECEMBER
Sean receives his final Christmas present from his father — an Akita puppy which the boy names Merry.

31 DECEMBER
'(Just Like) Starting Over' hits the top of the UK charts.

1981

JANUARY
The Israeli government reveals that a John Lennon Peace Forest will be planted near Safad.

EARLY JANUARY
Yoko sends Sean to Palm Beach with his nanny, so that he can get away from the morgue-like atmosphere surrounding their home. She begins work on completing 'Walking On Thin Ice', the rough mixes of which Lennon had been holding when he was shot.

5 JANUARY
'Woman' is selected on schedule as the second US 'Double Fantasy' single; there are few accusations of cashing-in, as Lennon had already been filmed for a promo clip for the single before his death.

7 JANUARY
'(Just Like) Starting Over' is succeeded by 'Imagine' as Britain's best-selling single.

11 JANUARY
Yoko issues a press statement, headed 'In Gratitude'.

"I thank you for your letters, telegrams and thoughts. They have come from all over the world... This was a consolation to me, since both John and I believed in brother and sisterhood that goes beyond race, color and creed.

"I thank you for your concern for people who are making money on John's name after his death. There are some of you who feel guilty about receiving paychecks for the Lennon articles you have written for the media. Do not feel guilty. People who wish to do business in a small scale in tribute to John, using his name but in good taste: you have my blessings.

"I thank you for your feeling of anger for John's death. I share your anger. I am angry at myself for not being able to protect John. I am angry at myself and at

all of us for allowing our society to fall apart to this extent.

"When John fell beside me, I felt like we were in a guerilla war, not knowing who or where the enemy was. I kept telling my staff, who were hiding razors and newspaper articles from me, to show me everything. I was in the dark. I had to know. I saw the death photo. John looked peaceful, like on the back of the 'Imagine' cover. Are you trying to tell me something, John? I saw the photo where he signed the autograph. Somehow that photo was harder for me to look at than the death photo. John's head was bent forward, obviously to sign his name. But it was a strange posture for John to show. Then I realized that he was signing for the gate of heaven.

"I felt that I owed this letter to you. This may not answer all your questions but it is the best I can do now. This is also in place of giving interviews, personal appearances, and private talks which many of you have asked for. I would like to have some time to myself.

"Remember, there's nothing you can do that can't be done. Imagine. Love, Yoko."

16 JANUARY
'Woman' reaches UK stores.

17 JANUARY
Fred Seaman travels to London, to deliver a video for the 'Woman' single to the BBC, for transmission on *Top Of The Pops*. He elects to take with him copies of Lennon's diaries for the second half of the Seventies, and give them to Julian – supposedly in accordance with John's personal wishes. By his account, he is tricked by a friend into proposing to construct a book out of the material in the Lennon manuscripts.

Seaman also hands over copies of unissued Lennon songs, which he has removed from the Dakota without Yoko's knowledge. He encourages Julian to record them.

18 JANUARY
The BBC begins broadcasting a six-part radio series, *The Lennon Tapes*, built around Andy Peebles' interview with the couple on 6th December.

1 FEBRUARY
Yoko Ono releases 'Walking On Thin Ice', the track which she and John had effectively completed less than an hour before his death. Its chilling mood of emotional withdrawal masking horrendous pain strikes an eerie note after the events of December 8. Even more confrontational is the B-side, 'It Happened', which opens with two minutes of dialogue between the Lennons, taped during the making of the 'Woman' video. "John Lennon, I can't believe it," Lennon quips at one point, as he sees the startled expression on a bystander's face; in February, this remark pre-empts the thoughts of most people who buy the record. The subsequent song seems to refer directly to the tragedy, although it was actually written and recorded in 1973.

5 FEBRUARY
Reports surface that the surviving Beatles are reuniting to record a tribute to Lennon.

8 FEBRUARY
Roxy Music issue a cover version of Lennon's 'Jealous Guy' as a tribute record; it tops the UK chart.

MARCH
Yoko Ono begins work on a solo LP in New York, with Phil Spector producing, after the musicians – basically the crew who performed on 'Double Fantasy' – refuse to take directions from Yoko. Spector's involvement proves to be brief, and Yoko takes back the project herself.

Yoko is also reported to be planning to launch a magazine called *Imagine*, to keep alive the guiding ideals of Lennon's life.

13 MARCH
Cash-in or celebration? Reactions are mixed as Lennon's entire performance with Elton

John from Madison Square Garden in November 1974 is issued as a UK single.

16 MARCH
The third US single from 'Double Fantasy' is released. Like 'Walking On Thin Ice', 'Watching The Wheels' seems to prefigure the tragedy in some way, taking on a new layer of poignancy after John's murder.

27 MARCH
UK release of 'Watching The Wheels'.

29 MARCH
A memorial service for Lennon is held at Liverpool's Anglican Cathedral, under protest from local Conservative politicians.

APRIL
The Lennons' publishing company, Lenono Music, is renamed Ono Music by Yoko.

16 APRIL
New York mayor Ed Koch signs a city ordinance renaming an area of Central Park close to the Dakota 'Strawberry Fields' in Lennon's memory.

21 APRIL
The *National Enquirer* claims that Lennon is still writing songs from beyond the grave, via psychic David Guardino. Among the 'new' compositions is 'To Be One Again', which calls for the remaining Beatles to re-form.

MAY
Lennon's bloodstained clothes are returned to the Dakota from the New York Coroner's office.

4 MAY
George Harrison releases a surprisingly jaunty tribute to his ex-colleague, 'All Those Years Ago'. The single becomes a 1981 Beatles reunion, as it features contributions from Paul McCartney and Ringo Starr.

22 MAY
Yoko Ono accepts a Handel Medallion, New York's highest medal of honour, on Lennon's behalf. "This city meant a lot to him," she says tearfully. "This was our town, and it still is."

8 JUNE
Yoko Ono's first album since Lennon's death, and her first solo LP since 1974, is released in the States. 'Season Of Glass' is packaged in a confrontational sleeve, which pictures Lennon's blood-stained spectacles in the window of their Dakota apartment. Yoko takes the photograph herself.

Like the packaging, the record itself arouses controversy, not least the chillingly disturbing 'No, No, No', which opens with the sound of gunshots and then chronicles a statement of extreme psychological and physical withdrawal.

12 JUNE
'Season Of Glass' is released in Britain.

15 JUNE
'The John Lennon Boxed Set' repackages Lennon's mainstream releases for Apple, from 'Live Peace In Toronto 1969' to 'Shaved Fish'. In keeping with many subsequent 'tributes', Lennon's avant-garde work with Yoko Ono is ignored.

MID-JUNE
Yoko and Lenono Music face plagiarism charges over the similarity between the 'Double Fantasy' song 'I'm Your Angel' and the 1928 standard 'Makin' Whoopee'.

22 JUNE
Mark Chapman pleads guilty to the second-degree murder of John Lennon.

JULY
Jack Douglas files a lawsuit against Yoko, claiming that he has received no royalties for his production work on 'Double Fantasy'. Yoko countersues, claiming fraud and misrepresentation.

6 JULY
Even in death, there is repackaging: Geffen reissue 'Starting Over' and 'Woman' as a double A-side in the States.

19 AUGUST
Yoko sends an open letter to friends and other possible benefactors, about the designation of an area of New York's Central Park as a memorial garden for John: "It will be known as Strawberry Fields. It happens to be where John and I took our last walk together. John would have been very proud that this was given to him, an island named after his song, rather than a statue or a monument.

"When we first met over ten years ago, we planted an acorn in England as a symbol of our love. We then sent acorns to all the heads of state around the world inviting them to do the same. So in the name of John and Yoko and the spirit of love and sharing, I would like once again to invite all countries of the world this time to offer plants rocks and/or stones of their nations for Strawberry Fields."

24 AUGUST
In a New York court, Mark David Chapman is sentenced to 20 years-to-life imprisonment, to be served in Attica State Prison.

26 AUGUST
Yoko picks the least radio-friendly track on 'Season Of Glass', the psychodramatic 'No, No, No', as a single.

19 SEPTEMBER
Paul Simon premières a tribute song to Lennon, 'The Late Great Johnny Ace', when he performs a reunion concert with Art Garfunkel in New York's Central Park, within view of the site of Lennon's murder. Bizarrely, his rendition of the song is interrupted when he is rushed by a fan shouting "Paul, I want to speak to you" on stage. Simon later confesses that he believed that, like Lennon, he was about to be murdered.

30 SEPTEMBER
A second single is released from Yoko's 'Season Of Glass': 'Goodbye Sadness'.

9 OCTOBER
On what would have been Lennon's 41st birthday, Yoko Ono announces: "October 9 has been proclaimed as International World Peace Day by the Foundation for World Peace. This was endorsed immediately by many organisations around the world. Keep wishing. Wishing is magic. Imagine all the people living life in Peace. Hope and Love, Yoko Ono Lennon."

In Los Angeles, a lifesize bronze statue of Lennon is unveiled at City Hall.

28 OCTOBER
Bob Eaton's biographical play *Lennon* opens at the Everyman Theatre in Liverpool.

NOVEMBER
Mark Chapman writes to Yoko, hinting that he is planning to write a book about his shooting of Lennon, and hoping that she will agree to support the project if he hands over all proceeds to charity.

9 NOVEMBER
More repackaging: another US Geffen single, coupling 'Watching The Wheels' and 'Beautiful Boy'.

DECEMBER
Julian Lennon complains that Yoko Ono is only giving him £150 a week from his father's estate. "Dad was always totally under her influence," he adds. "She has a lot of power. She is a bit scary, too."

7 DECEMBER
EMI 'celebrate' the first anniversary of Lennon's death (give or take a day or two) with 'The Beatles EP Collection', an expensive box set which features four supposedly exclusive stereo mixes.

8 DECEMBER
To mark the anniversary of Lennon's death, Yoko releases a short film of the couple walking in Central Park. In keeping with the Japanese rituals of mourning, she also crops some 30 inches off her hair.

1982

JANUARY
Yoko fires her assistant, Fred Seaman; he departs with Lennon manuscripts, diaries and recording equipment. Work continues apace on the plan for him, and several collaborators, to produce the definitive history of Lennon's final years, based on John's own day-by-day account. One of the plotters suggests that the diaries should be forged, so that Lennon can apparently 'support' Seaman's claim to be the closest courtier to the throne.

24 FEBRUARY
'Double Fantasy' is pronounced Album of the Year at the annual Grammy Awards. Yoko, and many of the gathered luminaries, weep as the presentation takes place.

MARCH
Yoko Ono is reported to have sold the rights to a forthcoming book about John Lennon to G.P. Putnam's for an estimated $5

million. The deal collapses when it emerges that she is required to offer any new book to Simon & Schuster, under the terms of her contract for *Grapefruit* back in 1970. Simon & Schuster are unwilling to match Putnam's offer, so Yoko abandons her literary plans.

1 MARCH
Rhino Records are forced to withdraw an album of novelty Beatles tributes, 'Beatlesongs', when Lennon fans object to the presence on the LP cover of a caricature of Mark Chapman.

8 MARCH
Perhaps the most effective of all the musical tributes to Lennon (bar Yoko's) is released – Elton John's 'Empty Garden (Hey Hey Johnny)'.

15 MARCH
The most stupid US Beatles single of all time, 'The Beatles Movie Medley', places the group's legacy at the mercy of cack-handed butchers.

22 MARCH
Another pointless piece of repackaging brings a compilation of Beatles film songs, 'Reel Music', into US stores.

29 MARCH
UK release date for 'Reel Music'.

19 APRIL
Queen become the latest artists to issue a tribute song to Lennon, 'Life Is Real (Song For Lennon)'.

20 APRIL
Yoko officially declares 'Strawberry Fields' open in Central Park.

26 APRIL
Paul McCartney pays musical tribute to his former partner, with the elegiac 'Here Today' on his 'Tug Of War' album.

24 MAY
'The Beatles Movie Medley' is thrown at the British public.

27 JUNE
Lennon's friend, Harry Nilsson, writes and records 'With A Bullet', a song designed to raise funds for the National Coalition To Ban Handguns. Nilsson has been heavily involved in the campaign since Lennon's death.

AUGUST
Yoko and the remaining Dakota staff uncover the extent of the thefts and deception carried out by Lennon's former aides and their accomplices. After much legal manoeuvring, all the missing documents but Lennon's 1980 diary are returned to Yoko.

Yoko and Sean join Elton John on stage at Madison Square Garden in New York, as Elton performs his Lennon tribute, 'Empty Garden'.

10 SEPTEMBER
After years of bootlegs, 12 tracks from The Beatles' Decca audition on January 1, 1962 finally appear on an 'official' (or semi-legal) LP. Omitted are the three Lennon/McCartney songs cut that day. Audiofidelity, who release the album, prove that their motives aren't entirely historical when they artificially extend the length of several songs on subsequent repackages of the material.

20 SEPTEMBER
Billy Joel includes his tribute song to Lennon, 'Scandinavian Skies', on his 'The Nylon Curtain' LP. Critics note that the entire album bears a heavy Lennon influence.

3 OCTOBER
It's announced that Yoko Ono has left Geffen Records for Polygram, and taken the unreleased 'Double Fantasy' out-takes, known as the 'Milk And Honey' album, with her.

11 OCTOBER
It's the 20th anniversary of the first Beatles release on EMI, so the company prepare '20 Greatest Hits' – with slightly different track listings in Britain and America. On the same day, *The Ballad Of John And Yoko* collects together material about the Lennons from the files of

Rolling Stone magazine, plus newly commissioned essays by the magazine's writers.

29 OCTOBER
Time for another Beatles single, 'Searchin' ', taken from the Decca tapes.

1 NOVEMBER
Several weeks late, EMI issue a 20th anniversary single of 'Love Me Do'. It hits No. 4 in the UK charts, prompting subsequent re-releases of all the other original Beatles singles, as close to their anniversary date as possible.

Issued on the same day is a 'new' John Lennon single, a remix of 'Love' from the 1970 'Plastic Ono Band' sessions. It's there to promote the day's third Lennon-related release, 'The John Lennon Collection'. This retrospective LP mixes 11 Apple recordings (from 'Give Peace A Chance' to 'Stand By Me') with six of Lennon's seven tracks from 'Double Fantasy'. Packaged in a sleeve featuring photos taken just a couple of days before John's death, the album represents a reasonable tribute to his work – though the omission of 'controversial' songs like 'Cold Turkey' and 'Woman Is The Nigger Of The World' demonstrates that commercial considerations have figured ahead of artistic motives.

8 NOVEMBER
'The John Lennon Collection' is issued in America, albeit with two tracks sliced from the vinyl edition of the LP. On the same day, Yoko Ono releases a new single, the poignant 'My Man'.

29 NOVEMBER
'Happy Xmas (War Is Over)' is released as a single in the States, to tie in with the 'Collection' LP. Ironically, it's one of the two tracks cut from the US album.

On the same day, Yoko Ono releases her second album since John's death, 'It's Alright'. The back cover photo shows her and son Sean greeting the ghostly figure of Lennon; mother and child are named as "keepers of the wishing well". John makes a more corporeal appearance on the record, when a brief tape of him shouting Yoko's name is incorporated into the song 'Never Say Goodbye'.

3 DECEMBER
Yoko's 'My Man' single is released in Britain.

6 DECEMBER
In what seems to be becoming an annual tradition, EMI release another weighty box set, 'The Beatles Singles Collection'.

10 DECEMBER
Yoko's 'It's Alright' LP appears in the UK

25 DECEMBER
Yoko pens 'Surrender To Peace', a statement printed a month later by the *New York Times*. In it, she recalls her foundation of Nutopia with John in 1973, and describes the conceptual country's flag as "the white flag of surrender. A surrender to peace." She explains that John, "a man who surrendered to the world, life and finally to Universe", said at the time: "Don't worry, Yoko. One day we'll put the flag up there. You and I. I promise."

Yoko continues: "It is time for you to rise. It is you who will raise the flag. I feel that John and I, as a unit, have done our share. The rest of my life belongs to our son, Sean. Remember, We Are Family. You and I are Unity. Speak out of love and you need not fear. We will hear. America The Beautiful. Surrender To Peace. I love you. Yoko Ono Lennon."

1983

19 JANUARY
A play by James McLure entitled *The Day They Shot Lennon* is staged at the NJ Theater in Princeton, New York.

7 FEBRUARY
'Never Say Goodbye', with its briefest of vocal appearances from Lennon, becomes Yoko's new US single.

Yoko and Sean in Strawberry Fields, New York's Central Park.

21 MARCH
'Not Now John' is released by Pink Floyd as a belated tribute to Lennon.

APRIL
Publishers Simon & Schuster reveal that Fred Seaman has been paid a $90,000 advance for a book about Lennon.

MAY
Former Beatles aide Peter Brown, namechecked in the song 'The Ballad Of John And Yoko', issues his book, *The Love You Make*, with poisonous 'revelations' about the Lennons' relationship.

6 MAY
Mike Oldfield's 'Moonlight Shadow', another tribute song for Lennon, is released.

27 MAY
Fred Seaman pleads guilty to grand larceny charges, and is sentenced on July 14 to five years' probation – on the condition that he never reveals the contents of the Lennon documents and manuscripts that had been in his possession.

JULY
Yoko Ono returns to the incomplete 'Milk And Honey' tapes from 1980, in preparation for releasing an album from the sessions.

6 JULY
The season of books throws up one of its oddest entries – *Dakota Days* by John Green, who was apparently Yoko Ono's Tarot card reader in the second half of the Seventies.

AUGUST
Simon & Schuster announce that they will not, after all, be publishing a book by Fred Seaman – who, instead, reveals his intention to aid Albert Goldman with his Lennon biography, in progress since 1981. In 1991, Seaman eventually publishes *John Lennon: Living On Borrowed Time* – a surprisingly detailed and convincing portrait of the Lennons, and his years with them.

13 SEPTEMBER
The Young Vic Theatre in London stages a play entitled *John, Paul, George, Ringo*.

9 OCTOBER
While a party is underway at the Dakota for Sean Lennon's 8th birthday, an intruder enters the building uttering threats against Yoko. He's merely the latest in a long succession of crank callers and mentally unstable individuals who have attempted to harass or attack Yoko and Sean since John's death.

DECEMBER
Marking the third anniversary of Lennon's death, Yoko Ono releases a new US album, 'Heart Play — Unfinished Dialogue'. It comprises 40 minutes of extracts from the interviews with the couple conducted by *Playboy*'s David Sheff in the months leading up to John's death. The fact that the LP appears on the same day as a new Paul McCartney album is, of course, a coincidence.

16 DECEMBER
'Heart Play' reaches UK stores.

1984

5 JANUARY
'Nobody Told Me', a brash, witty rocker, is released in the States as a new Lennon single, and a trailer for the 'Milk And Honey' LP.

9 JANUARY
UK release date for 'Nobody Told Me'.

19 JANUARY
'Milk And Honey', publicised as being the follow-up to 'Double Fantasy', is released in the USA. The cover photograph of the Lennons kissing is similar to the design of the 1980 LP, but the record actually mixes John's off-the-cuff demos from the start of the 'Fantasy' sessions with some post-1980 Yoko Ono performances.

27 JANUARY
'Milk And Honey' appears in Britain.

FEBRUARY
The March issue of *Playboy* magazine is published, with a feature by David Sheff entitled 'The Selling Of John Lennon'. The article reveals for the first time the details of Fred Seaman's theft of Lennon's diaries and work tapes from the Dakota, and the numerous threats made to Yoko and Sean since John's death.

13 FEBRUARY
Capitol Records celebrates the 20th anniversary of The Beatles' first US visit by reissuing 'I Want To Hold Your Hand'.

9 MARCH
'Borrowed Time' is issued in Britain as the follow-up to 'Nobody Told Me'.

15 MARCH
In the States, 'I'm Stepping Out' is the new Lennon single.

Yoko with Julian and Sean Lennon.

2 APRIL
Yoko Ono is ordered to pay 'Double Fantasy' co-producer Jack Douglas more than £1 million in unpaid royalties for the album, and also to give him royalties for his work on 'Milk And Honey'.

11 MAY
'Borrowed Time' is released in the States.

24 MAY
Tarot-card reader John Green publishes *Dakota Days*, intended as a controversial tell-all exposé of Lennon's final years. Fans snigger quietly.

JUNE
Random House publish *Come Together: John Lennon In His Own Time*, Jon Wiener's remarkable examination of Lennon's political life. It includes much new evidence about the US government's campaign to have Lennon deported in the early Seventies, retrieved from official FBI files.

The US record label Silhouette Music release 'Reflections & Poetry', featuring extracts from Lennon's RKO Radio interview on the day of his death, plus tapes of him reading poems from the mid-Sixties.

28 JUNE
Ray Coleman's biography, *John Winston Lennon 1940-1966*, wins critical plaudits for its fair and accurate portrayal of the Beatle's early life.

15 JULY
Geffen Records in Britain belatedly issue 'I'm Stepping Out' as the third single from 'Milk And Honey'.

13 SEPTEMBER
'Every Man Has A Woman', the compilation of Yoko Ono songs apparently planned by Lennon as a 50th birthday present for Yoko, is released in the States. It contains one previously unheard Lennon performance, of the title track – sung by Yoko on 'Double Fantasy'. The album also marks the musical début of the couple's young son, Sean.

21 SEPTEMBER
UK release date for 'Every Man Has A Woman'.

5 OCTOBER
Lennon's recently issued 'Every Man Has A Woman' track becomes a US single.

15 OCTOBER
John's son Julian Lennon releases his first solo LP, 'Valotte', which is predictably greeted with media comparisons between Julian and his father. But the first single from the album, 'Too Late For Goodbyes', becomes a worldwide hit.

30 OCTOBER
The second volume of Ray Coleman's definitive biography, *John Ono Lennon 1967-1980*, is published.

16 NOVEMBER
UK release date for the 'Every Man Has A Woman' single.

DECEMBER
Pressure from the individual Beatles forces EMI to scrap 'Sessions', an album of previously unissued material by the group. Bootleggers rub their hands in glee.

7 DECEMBER
An unpublished interview with John and Yoko from the summer of 1971, conducted by Peter McCabe and Robert Schonfeld, is published in the book *John Lennon: For The Record*.

8 DECEMBER
The anniversary of Lennon's death is marked in Britain by the TV screening of a new documentary film, *Yoko Ono: Then And Now*.

9 DECEMBER
Lennon biographer Ray Coleman unveils a memorial bench to the ex-Beatle in Edinburgh's East Princes Street Gardens.

1985

MID-FEBRUARY
Yoko Ono, George Harrison and Ringo Starr file a lawsuit against Paul McCartney, alleging that he has secretly increased his royalty rate for The Beatles' records without informing the others.

MARCH
Genesis Publications issues Derek Taylor's autobiography, *Fifty Years Adrift*, which includes reproductions of many letters and postcards sent to him by John. Another new book is *Listen To These Pictures: Photographs Of John Lennon*, collecting more than 100 photos taken between 1971 and 1980 by their friend Bob Gruen.

4 APRIL
The British press is seized by rumours that The Beatles are about to re-form, with Julian Lennon taking his father's place. Nothing happens.

13 MAY
British Rail name a new Pullman locomotive *John Lennon* in a ceremony at Liverpool's Lime Street Station.

25 JUNE
Actor Mark Lindsay is dropped from the cast of NBC-TV's movie *John And Yoko: A Love Story*. He had been slated to star as John Lennon, but is dismissed when Yoko Ono discovers that his real name is Mark Chapman.

29 JUNE
Lennon's psychedelically-decorated Rolls-Royce limousine is auctioned by Sotheby's in New York, for $2.2 million.

10 AUGUST
Ownership of the Lennon/McCartney song catalogue, handled by Northern Songs, passes to Michael Jackson, for around £34 million.

20 SEPTEMBER
During archive retrieval for an upcoming US radio project, 20 previously unpublished John Lennon songs are copyrighted in the States – credited as having all been written in 1980, though they actually date back as far as 1975. They include two numbers which are mistakenly attributed to Lennon, Grapefruit's 'Lullaby' and the Futz's 'Have You Heard The Word'.

3 OCTOBER
Another Lennon photographic portfolio is published, this one collecting pictures taken by mid-Seventies Beatles cameraman Dezo Hoffmann.

4 OCTOBER
Elton John issues his second tribute song to Lennon, an instrumental called 'The Man Who Never Died'.

9 OCTOBER
On what would have been Lennon's 45th birthday, New York authorities officially dedicate 'Strawberry Fields' in Central Park. Yoko and Sean perform the opening ceremony.

11 NOVEMBER
An edited version of John and Yoko's 1971 movie *Imagine* is released on home-video by EMI.

18 NOVEMBER
To capitalise on the publicity for the *Imagine* movie, EMI issues 'Jealous Guy' as a single.

22 NOVEMBER
Yoko Ono issues her third solo album since John's death, 'Starpeace'.

2 DECEMBER
The sentimental, bowdlerised but still sometimes moving TV film *John And Yoko: A Love Story* is premièred on NBC-TV.

6 DECEMBER
John Lennon: A Journey In The Life, starring actor Bernard Hill in the title role, is BBC TV's tribute to the ex-Beatle.

8 DECEMBER
On the fifth anniversary of Lennon's death, BBC radio broadcast a one-hour tribute, telling his story through extracts from his interviews.

1986

23 JANUARY
Lennon sons Sean and Julian jointly induct Elvis Presley into the Rock'n'Roll Hall Of Fame, in John's memory.

24 JANUARY
John Lennon: Live In New York City, a home-video and tie-in album, provides a first official release for material from the 1972 One To One concerts. The tapes for the releases are remixed by Yoko, who deliberately obscures her own vocals, omits several of her songs, and also smoothes out the raw intensity of Lennon's original performances.

24 FEBRUARY
The *Live In New York City* releases reach Britain.

28 FEBRUARY
Yoko Ono begins her first solo world tour in Brussels, Belgium. The US leg of the tour is soon cancelled because of poor ticket sales.

24 MARCH
Julian Lennon issues his second solo album, 'The Secret Value Of Daydreaming'.

MAY
Many of Lennon's sketches and lithographs are featured in an art exhibition, This Is My Story Both Humble And True, which goes on show in California.

17 JUNE
Musicians from Elephant's Memory file lawsuits against Yoko Ono, complaining that they had originally donated their performances at the One To One concerts to charity, and that they are receiving no royalties from the use of their playing on the 'Live In New York City' album and video.

6 OCTOBER
Skywriting By Word Of Mouth, a collection of Lennon stories, poems and articles mostly dating from 1975 and afterwards, is published around the world. The book demonstrates that Lennon had lost none of the verbal facility he demonstrated in his first two volumes from the mid-Sixties, but most critical comment centres on 'The Ballad Of John And Yoko', an autobiographical piece said to have been intended as a programme note for the Lennons' unfinished musical of the same name.

27 OCTOBER
Another posthumous Lennon album is released in the States. 'Menlove Avenue' mixes out-takes from the 1973/74 sessions for the 'Rock'N'Roll' album with rehearsals for the 'Walls And Bridges' LP from 1974. The cover art is provided by Andy Warhol.

3 NOVEMBER
UK release date for 'Menlove Avenue'.

1987

26 FEBRUARY
The first batch of Beatles CDs are released, part of a year-long campaign that returns all the group's original albums to the charts on both sides of the Atlantic.

MARCH
Yoko Ono allows film producer David Wolper access to her archives, in his quest to make "the definitive motion picture about the professional and private life of John Lennon", provisionally titled *In My Life*.

9 MARCH
Lennon is posthumously inducted into the US Songwriters Hall Of Fame; Yoko picks up the award.

27 MARCH
Footwear manufacturers Nike begin running US TV ads using The Beatles' 'Revolution' as the soundtrack. Fans are outraged by this use of Lennon's political anthem, though the advert is sanctioned by Yoko Ono.

4 APRIL
Yoko presents the first 'John Lennon New Age Award' to rock promoter Bill Graham at a New York ceremony.

24 APRIL
Sadler's Wells in London is the venue for the world première of *The Dream Is Over*, a ballet choreographed by Christopher Bruce to music from the 'John Lennon Plastic Ono Band' album.

1 JUNE
Beatlemania is revived one more time, as the 'Sgt. Pepper' CD marks the 20th anniversary of the album's original release, and prompts worldwide retrospectives from journalists of a certain age.

10 SEPTEMBER
Macmillan publish *The Lennon Companion*, an anthology of articles about the ex-Beatle and his work, which reprints several of the most famous Sixties interviews with John.

1988

18 JANUARY
The first edition of *The Lost Lennon Tapes*, an alternately fascinating and aggravating US weekly radio series, is made available for broadcast by the Westwood One network. Around 300 hours of rare Lennon recordings are apparently made available to the network, though these are carefully doled out in minuscule batches in each programme, outweighed by over-familiar and sometimes irrelevant material.

20 JANUARY
The Beatles are inducted into the Rock'N'Roll Hall Of Fame in New York. Lennon is represented by Yoko, Sean and Julian, but Paul McCartney refuses to attend because of the outstanding litigation between himself and the other Beatles. Yoko is also absent, though she slyly tells the press that John would have been there if he were still alive.

22 AUGUST
Beatles fans are duly outraged, as Albert Goldman's book *The Lives Of John Lennon* suggests that their hero was a murderer, an incapable drug addict and an unstoppable womaniser – when he wasn't kicking his baby son around the room or screwing The Beatles' manager. Despite its sensationalism, however, Goldman's tome is not the badly researched exploitation exercise that the fans are protesting against, although much of its speculation is quite absurd.

8 SEPTEMBER
An altogether kinder image of Lennon emerges from *John Lennon: My Brother*, written by his half-sister Julia Baird with assistance from Geoffrey Guiliano.

14 SEPTEMBER
Westwood One Special Report: Yoko's Response, a US networked radio show, allows Yoko to comment on Albert Goldman's biography.

19 SEPTEMBER
'Jealous Guy' is released as a US John Lennon single for the first time.

30 SEPTEMBER
John is honoured with a 'star' on Hollywood's Walk Of Fame on Sunset Boulevard – in front of the Capitol Records building.

4 OCTOBER
A new documentary film, *Imagine: John Lennon*, is premièred in New York, with Yoko Ono in attendance. The movie is an authorised 'biography' of the man, told through his own interview quotes, and featuring many previously unseen clips from Lennon/Ono films and home movies.
    On the same day, a double-LP of the same name is released, featuring one previously unheard Lennon song – 'Real Love' from 1980. And there's a tie-in book, comprising photos of John and quotes from him.

10 OCTOBER
UK release date for the 'Imagine: John Lennon' LP set.

25 OCTOBER
Yoko Ono and Cynthia Lennon attend the UK premiere of *Imagine: John Lennon*.

28 NOVEMBER
'Imagine' is re-released as a double A-side single with 'Jealous Guy' in Britain.

26 DECEMBER
Sean Ono Lennon makes his acting début, at the age of 13, in Michael Jackson's fantasy movie, *Moonwalker*.

1989

27 MARCH
Album No. 3 for Julian Lennon: 'Mr. Jordan'.

1 APRIL
Eighteen years after it was made, the Lennons' *Ten For Two* film of their late 1971 concert appearance is premièred in Detroit.

28 APRIL
The video release *Sweet Toronto* makes the entire Plastic Ono Band performance from Toronto in September 1969 available for the first time.

28 NOVEMBER
George Harrison tells a reporter that there will be no Beatles reunion "so long as John Lennon remains dead".

1990

1 JANUARY
It's Greening Of The World (GOW) year, according to Yoko Ono, who announces 12 months of environmental campaigns and events to mark what would have been Lennon's 50th birthday.

20 MARCH
An exhibition of Yoko Ono's artwork and films opens at the Riverside Studios in West London. Over the next five weeks, a dozen Lennon/Ono movies are given a rare public showing.

5 MAY
At the Pier Head in Liverpool, Yoko Ono stages and introduces a concert in honour of John Lennon, to raise money for The Greening Of The World John Lennon Scholarship Fund. Numerous rock, pop, country and soul stars perform generally inadequate covers of Lennon's song, while Ringo Starr and Paul McCartney each donate a special film.

28 JUNE
Also in Liverpool, but this time nearby at the King's Dock, Paul McCartney performs a special medley of John Lennon songs during his concert there. The renditions of 'Strawberry Fields Forever', 'Help!' and 'Give Peace A Chance' on this current tour mark his first ever playing of Lennon compositions in public.

JULY
Rickenbacker Guitars announce the issuing of a special John Lennon signature electric guitar series.

13 SEPTEMBER
One of the poorest Lennon biographies to date, Sandra Shevey's *The Other Side Of Lennon*, is published.

6 OCTOBER
To mark the week of what would have been Lennon's 50th birthday, BBC Radio air the first of a series of 10 programmes entitled *In My Life: Lennon Remembered*. A book of the same title soon follows.

9 OCTOBER
More than 1,500 radio stations around the globe simultaneously broadcast John Lennon's 'Imagine' on his 50th birthday – 'The Day Of Love', as Yoko designates it. "I wanted to provide a way for John's fans to do something together, but, at the same time, I wanted it to be original and simple," she explains.

29 OCTOBER
Author John Robertson publishes the first in-depth study of Lennon's work, *The Art And Music Of John Lennon*. It's a work of genius, it says here.

30 OCTOBER
A four-CD compilation of previously released material, 'Lennon', is released in Britain. Though it includes the whole of his 'John Lennon/Plastic Ono Band' LP, it generally favours Lennon's least controversial and experimental material.

8 NOVEMBER
More Lennon volumes hit the stores — including Philip Norman's *Days In The Life: John Lennon Remembered*, Nishi F. Saimaru's *John Lennon: A Family Album*, and *Daddy Come Home: The True Story Of John Lennon And His Father* by John's 41-year-old stepmother, Pauline Lennon.

12 NOVEMBER
The BBC gets in on the act again, with *John And Yoko – The Interview*, comprising extracts from Andy Peebles' meeting with the Lennons in December 1980.

3 DECEMBER
John And Yoko: The Bed-In, an edited version of the Lennons' 1969 film of similar title, is released on home-video in Britain.

21 DECEMBER
A second, less spectacular Greening Of The World Concert is staged at the Tokyo Dome.

1991

JANUARY
Cynthia Lennon issues limited edition reproductions of a set of John's cartoons, on Apple Corps notepaper, drawn in 1968.

4 JANUARY
Sean, Yoko and Lenny Kravitz discuss updating 'Give Peace A Chance' as a response to the outbreak of the Gulf War. Over the next week, they tape a new recording of Lennon's peace anthem, with more than 20 notable pop and rock performers.

15 JANUARY
The revamped 'Give Peace A Chance' is released, credited to the Peace Choir.

28 JANUARY
The BBC refuses to play the Peace Choir single, as part of the Corporation's new policy of not airing anti-war material. Lennon's song obviously still retains its anti-establishment bite.

20 FEBRUARY
Lennon is posthumously presented with a Lifetime Achievement Award at the Grammy ceremony in New York. Yoko Ono receives the award on his behalf.

MAY
Yoko threatens court action against pop band EMF, whose 'Schubert Dip' album includes a recording of Mark Chapman reading lyrics from Lennon's 'Watching The Wheels'. EMF agree to remove the offending track from the record.

12 JULY
Professor Jon Wiener, author of the groundbreaking study of Lennon's political life, *Come Together*, wins a court battle in San Francisco, forcing the FBI to release their remaining 69 secret files on John Lennon. The FBI appeals, as the deportation/surveillance battle continues long after Lennon's death.

28 SEPTEMBER
Julian Lennon releases his fourth LP, 'Help Yourself'.

9 OCTOBER
Former aide Fred Seaman is the latest insider to issue a memoir of Lennon, *Living On Borrowed Time*, which proves to be surprisingly informative about Lennon's final years.

6 DECEMBER
Mimi Smith, John's aunt who was responsible for his upbringing from the age of four, dies in Poole at the age of 88.

12 DECEMBER
Mimi Smith is cremated in Poole, at a ceremony attended by Yoko Ono, Cynthia Lennon and Sean Lennon.

1992

MARCH
A new book, *ai: Japan Through John Lennon's Eyes*, collects together sketches from the exercise book Lennon compiled in the late 70s when he was learning the Japanese language.

2 MARCH
Yoko Ono releases a 6-CD boxed set, 'Onobox', which includes many of the tracks she recorded with Lennon between 1968 and 1980, some of them previously unreleased.

23 MARCH
After four years of increasingly barren returns, the US radio series *The Lost Lennon Tapes* finally comes to a close.

APRIL
The Hours And The Times, a remarkable independent film capturing the essence of Lennon's relationship with Brian Epstein, is screened as part of a gay movie festival in London.

1 MAY
Another Nike commercial with a Lennon connection offends fans: this time, 'Instant Karma!' is sanctioned by Yoko for a TV advert for running shoes.

23 JUNE
The FBI loses another round of its battle to prevent the disclosure of its final secret files on John Lennon. The Supreme Court sets a September 11 deadline for the handover. When the files are finally released to author Jon Weiner, he discovers that the US government's illegal surveillance of Lennon in the Seventies continued for several years after he dropped his political campaigns. "Since these were the pretext for the surveillance," Weiner notes, "it makes the whole project more unjustified, more of an abuse than ever."

5 OCTOBER
The John Lennon Video Collection brings together a mix of original promo clips for Lennon's singles, and newly assembled footage.

1993

SEPTEMBER
Paul McCartney reveals that during the making of his most recent single, 'C'mon People', "John's spirit was in the studio with us. We found ourselves singing it just like John. We couldn't help it. In the end, we just went with it."

OCTOBER
An Australian theatrical tribute to Lennon, *Looking Through A Glass Onion*, opens in London.

NOVEMBER
Lennon fans are, as ever, "appalled" by a Yoko Ono art exhibition in Los Angeles, titled Family Album (Blood Objects). On display are bronze replicas of the bullet-riddled shirt Lennon was wearing when he was shot, and his blood-stained spectacles.

1994

JANUARY
Yoko Ono's sound collage 'Georgia Stone', which includes brief extracts from one of Lennon's final interviews, is released on the John Cage tribute album, 'A Chance Operation'.

15 JANUARY
Lennon's close friend Harry Nilsson dies of heart failure at the age of 52.

19 JANUARY
Paul inducts John into the Rock'n'Roll Hall Of Fame in New York. Appearing in public with Yoko for the first time since Lennon's death, he reads an 'open letter' to John reminiscing about their meeting and their work together. He also confirms persistent rumours in recent weeks that the remaining Beatles are planning to work together again.

After the event, Yoko presents Paul with unissued demo tapes of several unfinished Lennon compositions, including 'Free As A Bird', 'Real Love' and 'Grow Old With Me'.

FEBRUARY
After considering all three Lennon songs, Paul McCartney, George Harrison and Ringo Starr work on turning the 'Free As A Bird' demo into a finished song – their first work in the studio together since 1970. The track is provisionally intended for use in the *Anthology* series of Beatles documentary videos, planned for screening at the end of 1995, though more likely to surface in 1996 or beyond.

The sessions take place at McCartney's home studio, The Mill, in Sussex; Jeff Lynne is apparently acting as executive producer.

McCartney: "It's crazy really, because when you think about a new Beatles record, it's impossible, because John is not around. But we managed to get a track of John's that is unreleased, and we just pretended that he had gone on holiday and said, 'Finish it up – I trust you!' That gave us a nice free feeling that we wouldn't worry about what he would think. So we just got on with it, and treated it like any old tune The Beatles used to do and I am quite proud of it."

128

MARCH
John Lennon responds to The Beatles reunion with excitement, according to the British tabloid press, who report that he has been contacting Yoko via a medium. Meanwhile, a British songwriter claims that he has been inspired to write 120 songs in recent months by John's spirit. Within a few weeks, US psychic Jason Leen reveals that the remarkably prolific Lennon has helped him compose 13 songs, and has even suggested musicians who could record them.

APRIL
Julian Lennon tells the London *Evening Standard* that he has been invited to contribute to the new Beatles sessions by Paul McCartney. "He asked if I fancied doing some music," Julian says, "which totally shocked me." But the liaison fails to take place.

22 JUNE
The surviving Beatles regroup for more sessions at The Mill, once again working on the unfinished Lennon song 'Free As A Bird'.

JULY
Julian Lennon is reported to be considering legal action against Yoko Ono, on the grounds that he has not received his due portion of his father's estate, which she controls.

15 SEPTEMBER
A recently discovered tape of two songs by The Quarry Men, taped on the day in July 1957 when Lennon first met Paul McCartney, is sold at Sotheby's for £70,000. The primitive-sounding tape of 'Putting On

The Style' and 'Baby Let's Play House' reveals the band as a raw skiffle unit, with Lennon already rasping like a natural born rock'n'roller. EMI eventually purchase the tape, with the approval of The Beatles' Apple company.

LATE OCTOBER
In a bizarre media event Yoko Ono covers the German town of Langenhagen with 70,000 posters of a naked bottom. "Faces can lie," she says. "Backsides can't."

30 NOVEMBER
The double-CD of BBC radio session recordings, 'Live At The BBC', becomes the group's first official release of 'new' material since 1977. The record goes straight to No. 1, provoking massive media coverage.

1995

22 FEBRUARY
Cynthia Lennon belatedly becomes the sixth member of the Lennon family to issue a record, as her début single, 'Those Were The Days', is released.

6 MARCH
Lennon's rendition of 'Baby It's You' is pulled from 'Live At The BBC' as a new Beatles single.

11 MARCH
A bizarre recording session at Paul McCartney's home studio links the McCartney and Lennon families in music. The day's work produces 'Hiroshima, It's Always A Beautiful Blue Sky', an Ono composition. Yoko takes lead vocal, supported by Paul

McCartney, who also contributes bass, and his daughters Mary, Heather and Stella. Meanwhile, Linda McCartney plays celeste, and Sean Lennon and Paul's son James McCartney play guitars. The experimental piece is intended to mark the 50th anniversary of the dropping of the first atomic bomb on the Japanese city of Hiroshima in 1945.
    Yoko Ono: "Montague and Capulet coming back together was beautiful. It was a healing for our families to come together in this way. That feeling was very special."
    Sean Lennon: "It's the result of our reconciliation after 20 years of bitterness and feuding bullshit. Here were these people who had never actually played together actually making music. It was incredible working with Paul."

15 MARCH
At a US press conference, Paul McCartney reveals more details about the recording sessions for the 'Free As A Bird' Beatles reunion: "It's spooky to hear John singing lead, but it's beautiful. People said beforehand we shouldn't do it, but that kind of focused us up a bit. It was a joyful experience. George played some great guitar, we did some beautiful harmonies – so much so that Ringo said, 'It sounds like the bloody Beatles'."

EARLY APRIL
It is revealed that Paul McCartney, George Harrison and Ringo Starr have been overdubbing a second John Lennon home demo, 'Real Love', as part of the *Anthology* project. This video history of

The Beatles, with tie-in single ('Free As A Bird') and rarities set, are scheduled for November release. But still delayed is another multi-CD package, meant to collect together the best out-takes and demos from Lennon's solo career, which has been in preparation since the start of the decade.

Top: Yoko with Sean and Paul McCartney at John's induction into the Rock'n'Roll Hall Of Fame, January 1994.